MAKING FABULOUS PINCUSHIONS

$\mathscr{P}$ MAKING FABULOUS
INCUSHIONS

93 Designs for Spectacular & Unusual Projects

Jo Packham

A STERLING/CHAPELLE BOOK
Sterling Publishing Co., Inc.   New York

For Chapelle Limited

Owner:
Jo Packham

Editor:
Leslie Ridenour

Staff:
*Sandra Anderson, Trice Boerens,
Malissa Boatwright,
Rebecca Christensen,
Holly Fuller, Cherie Hanson,
Holly Hollingsworth,
Susan Jorgensen, Susan Laws,
Amanda McPeck,
Tammy Perkins, Jamie Pierce,
Leslie Ridenour, Cindy Stoeckl,
Nancy Whitley, and Lorrie Young*

Pincushion Designers:
*Mary Boerens, Trice Boerens,
Sharon Ganske, Mary Jo Hiney,
Tammy Johnson, Susan Laws,
Jo Packham, Jamie Pierce,
Elsie Snyder, Karen Snyder and
Carolyn Taylor*

Photographer:
*Kevin Dilley
for Hazen Photography*

Reference:
       Colby, A. (1988). Pincushions. London: B T Batsford.

Library of Congress Cataloging-in-Publication Data

Packham, Jo.
       Making fabulous pincushions : 93 designs for spectacular and
unusual projects / by Jo Packham.
             p.   cm.
       "A Sterling/Chapelle book."
       Includes index.
       ISBN 0-8069-0994-3
       1. Pincushions. I. Title.
TT899.3.P33   1995   94-23821
746.9—dc20   CIP

10 9 8 7 6 5 4 3 2 1

A Sterling/Chapelle Book

Published by Sterling Publishing Company, Inc.
387 Park Avenue South, New York, N.Y. 10016
© 1995 by Chapelle Ltd.
Distributed in Canada by Sterling Publishing
℅ Canadian Manda Group, One Atlantic Avenue, Suite 105
Toronto, Ontario, Canada M6K 3E7
Distributed in Great Britain and Europe by Cassell PLC
Villiers House, 41/47 Strand, London WC2N 5JE, England
Distributed in Australia by Capricorn Link (Australia) Pty Ltd.
P.O. Box 6651, Baulkham Hills, Business Center, NSW 2153, Australia
Printed in Hong Kong
All Rights Reserved

Sterling ISBN 0-8069-0994-3

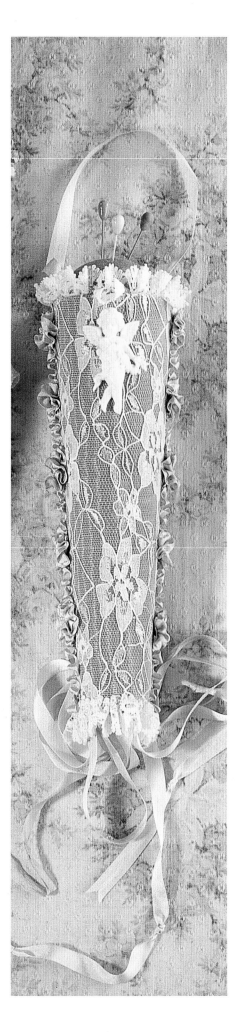

Dedication

Sara

There was so much to teach and so much to share and the time has traveled by so fast. So now that you are grown the time has come for me to say, "thank you," because the happiest moments my heart has known are those that were spent with you.

I love you.

Mom

Contents

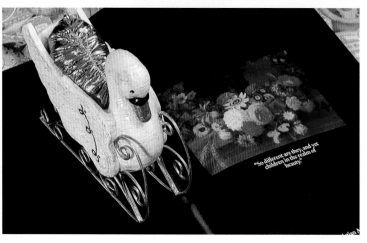

"So different are they, and yet
children in the realm of
beauty."

Introduction

Pincushions have graced virtually every sewing table that ever was. They have a splendid history and a charming manner.

Peek into a bygone era, as the tinkling bell at the door announces arrival and departure times of the daily patrons of the couturier's shop. Fine gentlemen and fashionable ladies examine the latest styles in the converted tea parlor, where textiles, scented of distant lands, sit stacked from the rug to the rafters. Over and between these fabricated cliffs, the sheerest laces fall and spill onto the floor, mixing with rattan baskets, treasuring notions, threads, and trinkets.

With measurements taken in front of a beveled mirror, enticing tales are exchanged in hushed voices. Squeals of delight and wisps of steam from chamomile tea accompany winsome anecdotes.

Observing all—amid dress forms, hat boxes, tapes, and scissors—a quiescent pincushion reposes on the mantle. Close at hand, the fat tuffet of velvet poised in a silver dish guards a myriad of sharp, shiny pins and needles. It is an integral part of the day's enterprise.

Although essential to the trade of the couturier and tailor throughout the past four centuries, pincushions have received little praise. We honor them here in these pages. With antique reproductions and contemporary ideas, some of these will become family heirlooms while others are perfect for making to sell or give away. We invite you to capture a bit of the past, and we hope that you will come up with your own ideas for creating fabulous pincushions.

Jo Packham

History

In the past, one never knew when a pin or needle would come in handy during the course of a busy day. And so it was necessary to carry them along. However, sharp objects do not sit well in unprotected pockets or loose in a pouch or purse. It became necessary to have them secured and kept to themselves.

Long before metal pins, the first sewing utensils were fashioned from sharp thorns and fish and animal bones. These were fragile and needed protection. And so, they were placed in a case. Native Americans used folded pieces of soft skins, called thorn cases.

The 1300s record small cases which were made to house pins and needles to be carried on a person or in a pouch or purse. These were made of bone, ivory, and silver. They were usually cylindrical and took upon them names such as pin keeper, pin-poppet, pin-case, and tuffet.

By the end of the 16th century, sewers used "pin pillows" of finely embroidered satin, canvas, and linen.

Drawstring purses used from the late 1500s to the early 1700s were accompanied by a matching pincushion that hung from the bag by a cord.

The 1700s saw the transition from pin pillows to mounted cushions. These were mounted on silver and wooden stands or found in the lid of a trinket box.

In the mid-1700s the pincushion, a seemingly undemonstrative tool of the tailor, suddenly became the medium of the voice of rebellion. Women showed their support for a cause by stitching a verse of political dissent or propaganda on the cushion, attaching it to a ribbon, and hanging it from their garter.

Historical events, such as the death of a member of royalty, were commemorated in the decoration of pincushions.

Pinwheels were designed to be carried in pockets. Some were made of cloth and were lightly decorated. Others were made of wood, ivory, mother-of-pearl, Tonbridge Ware, and leather.

Pin-stuck pincushions were all the rage from the 17th through the 19th centuries. These cushions were more decorative than useful. Their decoration was made up entirely of pins. The pins could not be removed without spoiling the pattern of the decoration.

These held great social significance and were used in courting, marriage, and maternity. Inscribed with messages of love, wishes for a newlywed couple, or the name and date of a child's birth, these keepsakes superceded social class and standing. No couple did without one for their new child.

Pin-stuck cushions with beads became very popular for decorating but were not very practical.

Pincushions were given as gifts and were valued as a status symbol. Any occasion was suitable for giving a pincushion.

The 19th-century parlour encouraged making pincushions for decor—usually wall hangings. Egg cups, baskets, ornamental china, wood, glass, and metal objects were fitted with pincushions. This was considered a silly time in art deco history.

Following this era, pincushions were used more as sewing aids than as knick knacks. There were many versions of clamp pincushions, but all consisted of decorative clamps which screwed onto a table and held fabric tight.

The weighted pincushion soon followed. Dressmakers didn't have time to be chasing fluffy pillows around the table to keep their pins.

People today seem to have a fascination with tools of the past. Vintage sewing things, such as pincushions, have become much sought after collectibles.

By combining nostalgia and sensibility, pincushions created today, like those found in this book, set new standards for excellence in artistry and yield satisfying results in efficiency.

Recovering an Old Pincushion

Recovering an old shabby cushion can dramatically improve the appearance of a cherished mount.

You can also create an original pincushion by exploring your own home. You may find a mount such as a porcelain shoe, an antique candy dish, or a favorite tea cup.

From the old pincushion, remove the cushion from its mount. Open it and retrieve any pins and needles that may have worked into it.

Choose your cover. Cushions, traditionally, have been made from velvet, satin, or embroidered linen. (However, ours take advantage of a wide variety of fabrics.)

Take measurements of your old or new mount to determine how much fabric is needed. The following formula will determine the diameter of a circular cushion:

width of mount + (depth of
mount + height above
mount x 2)

Sew a gathering stitch ¼" around your fabric circle. Pull threads until fabric cups. Stuff firmly. Pull threads tightly and tie off. Tuck raw edges inside and secure opening with small stitches through closure.

Fix the cushion in place and stitch or glue securely to mount.

Embellishments can come in the form of ribbon roses and rosettes, ribbon, charms, tulle, lace, cording, tatting, braid, buttons, beads, pearls — whatever!

Stuffing

Essentially, there are two kinds of stuffing used in pincushions— granular and fibrous.

Other components such as paper, cardboard, and lead serve as weights or stiffeners.

Granular Materials

Usually found in the form of bran, sawdust, and emery powder, granular materials, when used for pincushions, require special precautions. For instance, it is necessary to make a special cover to hold them as they tend to disintegrate and leak through fine, loosely woven fabrics.

Granular material must be very dry before stuffing. Otherwise, the pins will rust in their keeper.

Fibrous Materials

Fibrous materials are recommended most for stuffing pincushions.

Woolen fibers are best because they safeguard against rust.

This is the age of recycling— rethink, reuse, recycle. Old scraps of worn blanket and tweed can be unraveled for stuffing.

Unraveled knitting or crochet and woven woolen fabrics that seem to have lost their usefulness find new life in a pincushion.

Remnants of woven wool fabrics, such as flannel, tweed, and felt, can be stitched together in layers and trimmed to the shape of flat or box cushions.

For a rounded cushion, strips of wool fabric rolled up like a sweet roll provide form and function.

Synthetic fabrics should be avoided. Often disintegrating, foam rubber has a short life. Cotton wool, characteristically hard and lumpy, is also unappealing for use as a stuffing.

For convenience and ease, many projects in this book call for a Styrofoam ball, cone, or egg.

Stuffing Helps

When trying to fill out corners and curves, reach for your stuffing stick. Anything from a skewer to a knitting needle to a crochet hook will serve well—just take care not to poke holes in the fabric.

A wide-necked funnel is useful when pouring granular stuffing. It fits easily in a small opening and helps avoid messes.

Tailor weights, small bags of shot, heavyweight cardboard, or lightweight cardboard placed in the bottom center of your pincushion will help keep it upright and stationary.

Washed and tested fabric takes a pin more easily.

Fancy Pins

Bee

MATERIALS
Hat-pin blank
1" of ¼" cord
1" of 1" yellow wired ribbon
1½" of ⅝" gold-mesh wired
    ribbon
2 black artificial stamens
Hot glue gun and glue sticks

DIRECTIONS
1. Stick hat-pin blank through center of cord and hot-glue to secure. Stick hat-pin blank through center of yellow ribbon length.

2. Wrap and glue yellow ribbon length around cord. Pinch and glue one end closed. Place stamens in other end and pinch and glue closed.

Diagram

3. On one raw end of gold-mesh ribbon, fold and glue corners back, forming a point. Fold and glue point back. Repeat on opposite end. Pinch in center and glue to back of bee; see Diagram.

Ribbon and Beads

MATERIALS
3½" soft sculpture needle or hat-pin blank
Assorted beads
⅛" silk ribbon in assorted colors
Super glue

DIRECTIONS
1. Super-glue one small bead to top of soft sculpture needle.

2. Cut ribbon in 4" to 6" pieces. Gather ribbon on needle by piercing through center at ½" to ¾" intervals. Push ribbon up tightly.

3. Add more beads. Finish with small bead at bottom. Super-glue.

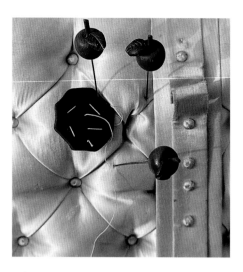

Apple

MATERIALS
½" wooden apple
Hat-pin blanks
Toothpick
Small amount of sculpting clay
Acrylic paints: red, brown, green
Paintbrush
Super glue
Drill and small drill bit

DIRECTIONS
1. Paint wooden apple red. Highlight with brown.

2. For apple stem, cut toothpick into ½" piece, paint brown and glue with super glue to top of apple.

3. Form small leaf with sculpting clay. With a pin or sharp knife, make veins in leaf. Set according to manufacturer's instructions. Paint leaf green and veins brown. Glue to top of apple.

4. Drill hole ¼" in apple bottom. Super-glue to pin top.

Carrot

MATERIALS
Sculpting clay
Hat-pin blank
Moss (greenery)
Acrylic paints: orange and brown
Paintbrush
Super glue

DIRECTIONS
1. From sculpting clay, knead one-quarter section until soft. Roll into ball. Roll on hard surface to make a cone/carrot shape about 1½" long.

2. Push hat-pin blank ½" into pointed end of carrot. Remove pin, leaving a hole in center of carrot. Use pin to make indentations in sides of carrot.

3. Place carrot on foil-covered cookie sheet. Bake at 275° F for 1 hour or until hard. Let cool.

4. Paint orange. With small brush, highlight indentations on sides with brown paint.

5. Super-glue pin in end. Super-glue small amounts of moss to carrot top.

Lady Bug

MATERIALS
Unfinished wooden plug
Hat-pin blank
Acrylic paints: red, black, white
Super glue
Drill and small drill bit

DIRECTIONS
1. Drill very small hole in center bottom of wooden plug.

2. Cut off top of hat-pin blank. Glue pin in hole of plug. Let dry.

3. Paint entire top of plug red. Paint bottom of plug black. Let dry.

4. Using black, paint a half circle on one edge of plug for head. From center of half circle, paint a straight black line to opposite side of plug, breaking off into a V. Fill in V with black paint.

Diagram

5. With a small thin paintbrush, paint antennas from head. Using a straight pin with a small head, dip in black paint and make three dots on each side of the straight line. Dip pin in white paint and dot on two eyes. Let dry. With pin tip, dip in black and make small dots inside white eyes; see Diagram.

Bullion Petal Stitch

1. Using one strand of embroidery floss, bring needle up at 1, down at 2, with a loose stitch. Bring needle top out again at 1; do not pull needle completely through the fabric.

2. Wrap floss loosely around needle about thirteen times. Holding finger over coiled floss, pull needle through wrapped floss. Insert needle again at 2, pulling to fabric back. If desired, pull floss slightly to curve bullion petal.

3. Stitch petal groups, forming rose as desired.

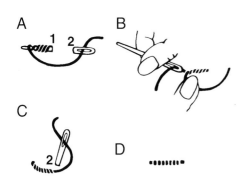

Cascading

Bow variation: With ribbon length, tie a small bow. Thread needle with tails. Ribbon-stitch to fabric very loosely, twisting ribbon between each stitch; place stitches as desired.

Ribbon length variation: Repeat, omitting bow.

Couching

These stitches are used to anchor a ribbon length to fabric. With embroidery floss or ribbon, bring needle up at 1, down at 2. Repeat to attach ribbon length as desired.

Fabric Leaf/Petal

1. Fold a 2" fabric circle in half, with raw edges aligned. For a crisper leaf/petal, press fabric.

2. With folded edge up, fold into thirds, overlapping sides with raw edges aligned.

3. Stitch running thread on raw edge. Gather tightly. Wrap thread around stitches to secure.

Ribbon variation: For ribbon leaf/petal, overlap ends and stitch. Trim excess.

Fabric/Ribbon Rose

1. Fold fabric strip in half lengthwise with long, raw edges aligned. For a crisper rose, press fabric.

2. Fold fabric ends at right angles. Stitch gathering thread on long raw edge, leaving needle and thread attached.

3. Gather fabric slightly, simultaneously wrapping to make flower. Force needle through lower fabric edge; secure thread. Trim excess. Fluff.

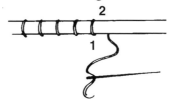

Fabric Yo-Yo

Fold raw edges of a 2½" fabric circle under ¼", sewing a gathering stitch on outer edge. Gather tightly. Knot ends to secure. Slightly flatten puckered circle, placing tightened gathers to center. The smooth side is bottom and gathered side top.

Fern Stitch

Using ribbon length, work from top to bottom of front, bringing needle up at 1, down at 2. Bring needle up at 3, down again at 1. Bring needle up at 4, down again at 1. Repeat, until desired length is achieved.

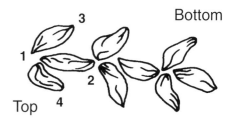

Fluting

Fluting is usually used as a border. Attach one ribbon end to fabric, loop to desired length, and glue. Repeat, making a series of even loops.

French Knot

Using one strand of embroidery floss or ribbon length, bring needle up at 1. Wrap floss/ribbon around needle two times. Insert needle a short distance from 1, pulling floss/ribbon until it fits snugly around needle. Pull needle through to back.

Gathered Circle

1. Fold ribbon in half with right sides facing and edges aligned. Stitch ends.
2. Sew gathering thread on one long edge. Gather tightly; secure thread. Flatten.

Lazy-Daisy Stitched Leaf/Bud

Using indicated number of strands of embroidery floss or ribbon length, bring needle up at 1, down at 2, with a loose stitch. Bring needle up on one side of floss/ribbon at 3, then back through fabric on opposite side at 4. A bud is often finished at 1 and 2 by a French knot.

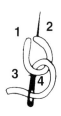

Ribbon Stitch

Using ribbon length, bring needle down at 1, up at 2, down at 3; repeat as desired.

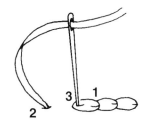

Ribbon Leaf

1. Fold ribbon length in half lengthwise, with long, wired edges aligned. Turn folded ribbon corners up to within 1/8" from wired edge.
2. Stitch running thread. Gather; secure ends. Open and shape leaf.

Ribbon Loops

1. With a dressmaker's pen, mark 1/2" allowance on each end of ribbon. Measure and mark loop length from first mark, as shown, adjusting for length and number of loops, as indicated in directions, with 3/8" between each loop.
2. Beginning at one end, fold ribbon, aligning 1 to 2. Stitch gathering thread through aligned marks. Gather tightly. Wrap thread around stitches to secure. Repeat with remaining marks to form additional loops.

Knotted variation: Mark ribbon as below; then mark center of each loop. Knot ribbon loosely at center marks. Tie all knots first; then stitch as below.

Ribbon/Fabric Rosette

1. For 1/8" rosette, cut 5" ribbon length; for 1/4" rosette, cut 9" length. Mark center of ribbon length. Beginning at one end, fold end forward at right angle. Holding vertical length, begin rolling ribbon at fold horizontally to form bud.
2. Then, fold horizontal ribbon backward at right angle and continue rolling bud, aligning top edges of bud to second fold (rounding corner).
3. Continue folding ribbon backward at right angles and rolling bud to center mark. Secure, leaving needle and thread attached.
4. Stitch gathering thread on edge of remaining ribbon length. Gather tightly. Wrap gathered ribbon around bud. Secure and fluff flower.

Layered variation: Layer lengths of ribbon. Handling as one, fold and stitch as below.

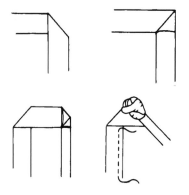

Beadwork

To attach beads to fabric, bring needle up at 1, through bead and down at 2 (lower left to upper right). Secure, bringing needle up at 3, through bead and down at 4 (lower right to upper left).

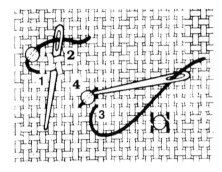

Blanket Stitch

The blanket stitch is used as an edging for surface embroidery. Pretty and practical, this stitch takes in the hem while it decorates. Begin thread on back of design with a backstitch. Bring thread to front of design, hold down loop and insert needle at 1 (just beyond hem line); then bring needle out and through loop at 2. Repeat, making evenly spaced stitches until design is complete.

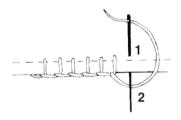

Cardboard

Heavyweight cardboard is rigid, yet can be cut with scissors, and is used for foundation shapes such as bases, lids and trays. Lightweight cardboard is bendable and is used to mold around foundation shapes.

Clipping Curves/Trimming Corners

Allowances on corners, curves or points should be clipped to create ease and reduce bulk. Clip into allowance at intervals of either ¼" or ½", cutting to, but not through, the stitching.

Cross-stitch Tips

Cross-stitch: Make one cross-stitch for each symbol on chart. Bring needle up at A, down at B, up at C, down at D; see Diagram. For rows, stitch across fabric from left to right to make half-crosses, then back to complete stitches.

Diagram

Fabrics: Designs in this book are worked on even-weave fabrics made especially for cross-stitch, which can be found in most needlework shops. Fabrics used for models are identified in sample informations by color, name, and thread count per inch.

Preparing fabric: Cut fabric at least 3" larger on all sides than finished design size or cut as indicated in sample information to ensure enough space for project assembly. To keep fabric from fraying, whipstitch or machine-zigzag along raw edges or apply liquid ravel preventer.

Needles: Choose a tapestry needle that will slip easily through fabric holes without piercing fabric threads. For fabric with 11 or fewer threads per inch, use needle size 24; for 14 threads per inch, use needle size 24 or 26; for 18 or more threads per inch, use needle size 26. Never leave needle in design area of fabric. It may leave rust or a permanent impression on fabric.

Finished design size: To determine size of finished design, divide stitch count by number of threads per inch of fabric. When design is stitched over two threads, divide stitch count by half the threads per inch.

Floss: Use 18" lengths of floss. For best coverage, separate strands. Dampen with wet sponge. Then put back together number of strands called for in color code.

Stitching method: For smooth stitches, use push-and-pull method. Starting on wrong side of fabric, bring needle straight up, pulling floss completely through to right side. Re-insert needle and bring it back straight down, pulling needle and floss completely through to back of fabric. Keep floss flat but do not pull thread tight. For even stitches, tension should be consistent throughout.

Gathering Stitch

Using thread, bring needle in and out of fabric in loose ¼" intervals, leaving long tails for gathering. If preferred, where appropriate, machine-stitch.

Glue

When gluing is referred to in projects, use tacky glue or a hot glue gun and glue sticks to attach embellishments. For boxes, when gluing fabric to cardboard, see "Laminating" below.

Laminating

Supplies:
Paper (to cover work surface)
3" disposable paint roller
Paint tray
Tacky glue

1. Pour glue in paint tray. (It is important to keep hands free of glue while laminating; a damp rag may be useful.)
2. Place cardboard on covered work surface. Saturate paint roller with glue, rolling on paint tray to remove excess. Roll a thin coat of glue on surface of cardboard as indicated in directions.
3. Place cardboard, glue side down, on wrong side of fabric. Turn, smoothing fabric over cardboard with hand. Glue raw edges to back. Shape laminated cardboard while still pliable and before it is completely dry.

Marking On Fabric/Ribbon

Mark on fabric/ribbon with an air or water-soluble dressmaker's pen. If project cannot be washed, use an air-soluble pen. All pens leave a small amount of residue.

Patterns

Supplies:
Dressmaker's pen
Tracing paper

1. Transfer patterns and information to tracing paper. Some patterns are reduced to fit on a page.
2. Patterns which are a reduction of the original size should be enlarged to indicated percentage using a photocopy machine. It is best to use a professional copy center as some copiers are not capable of of enlarging to some indicated percentages.

Seam Allowance

Before cutting fabric, add ¼" to ½" seam allowance to patterns.

Slipstitch

With a needle and thread, make small, almost invisible stitches. Slipstitching is used to secure a folded edge to a flat surface.

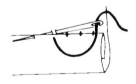

Scoring

Supplies:
Ruler/straight edge
Pencil

1. Score cardboard, according to directions; dotted lines on patterns indicate scoring.
2. With ruler as a guide, lightly cut halfway through cardboard with utility knife. The cardboard will bend easily with the cut side out.

Tack

To tack fabric or trim is to join two or more layers with small, inconspicuous hand stitches.

Tea Dye

Supplies:
8 tea bags
Large bowl
Muslin
Tongs

1. Place tea bags in bowl. Boil enough water to fill bowl one-third to halfway full. Steep tea bags in water until reaches desired shade.
2. Let tea cool for a few minutes.
3. Twist muslin. Using tongs, submerge muslin in tea. Dye to desired shade.
4. Remove from tea and rinse thoroughly. Air-dry dyed muslin.

Whipstitch

Whipstitch is usually used to join two finished edges, but it can also be used to secure an edge to a background fabric. Using a single strand of thread (unless otherwise indicated) knotted at one end, insert needle at 1, pick up a few threads of both layers of fabric, bringing it out at 2.

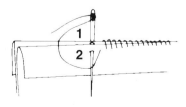

Chapter
One
Vintage

Victorian Scrolling

Part	Description	Dimensions	Quantity
A	Back	11" x 9" x ¼"	1
B	Shelf	9" x 3" x ¼"	1
C	Brace	1½" x ⅝" x ¼"	1
D	Cushion Backing	2⅛" x ½" x ¼"	1
E	Bottom Design Edge	5⅝" x 1⅞" x ¼"	1
F	Top Design Panel	1⅞" x ⅝" x ¼"	1
G	Ornamental Metal Pin	½" diameter x ⅜"	2
H	Cushion Mount	2⅝" x 2" x ⅛"	1
I	Design Circles	1¼" diameter x ⅛"	2
J	Hooks	¼" diameter	2

MATERIALS

Parts A through J described above
Wood recommendations:
  Bird's Eye Maple for parts A, B, C, and E
  Dark East Indian Rosewood for parts F, H, and I
Wood stain and/or varnish
3" x 4" piece of fabric for pincushion
7" piece of braid trim
One 3" Styrofoam oval cut in half lengthwise
Scrap of fleece
4" piece of ¼" wood dowel
Wooden thread spool
One small screw and several finishing nails
Wood glue
Wood carving tool
Clamp
Scroll Saw
Band Saw

DIRECTIONS

WARNING: This design has many sharp curves. Be careful not to torque scroll saw blade, which could result in breaking the blade and causing injury.

1. Using a photocopy machine, enlarge patterns on page 22 to 200%.

2. Draw patterns A, B, C, and E onto wood. Cut out excess wood away from patterns. Draw starting holes into blank areas and scroll saw pattern. We recommend cutting part E inside pattern first and then assemble with wood glue and clamp onto part A. After this is dry, cut the inside pattern of part A.

3. Cut out parts D, F, and H with band saw.

4. Cut out circles (I) from a 1¼"-diameter dowel and notch V cuts around them with a wood carving tool.

5. Stain or varnish wood as desired.

6. Glue a double cushion of fleece onto the half Styrofoam oval. Cover oval with fabric, gluing excess material onto back. Glue cushion onto part D. Glue braid trim around edge. Screw on from back of part A with part H in between.

7. Use ornamental metal pins (G) to attach F to A.

8. Assemble using a thin layer of wood glue between parts. Parts B and C may be nailed from behind with finishing nails to give strength to the shelf.

9. Screw hooks (J) into circles (I).

10. Place wood dowel through holes in C and thread spool onto dowel.

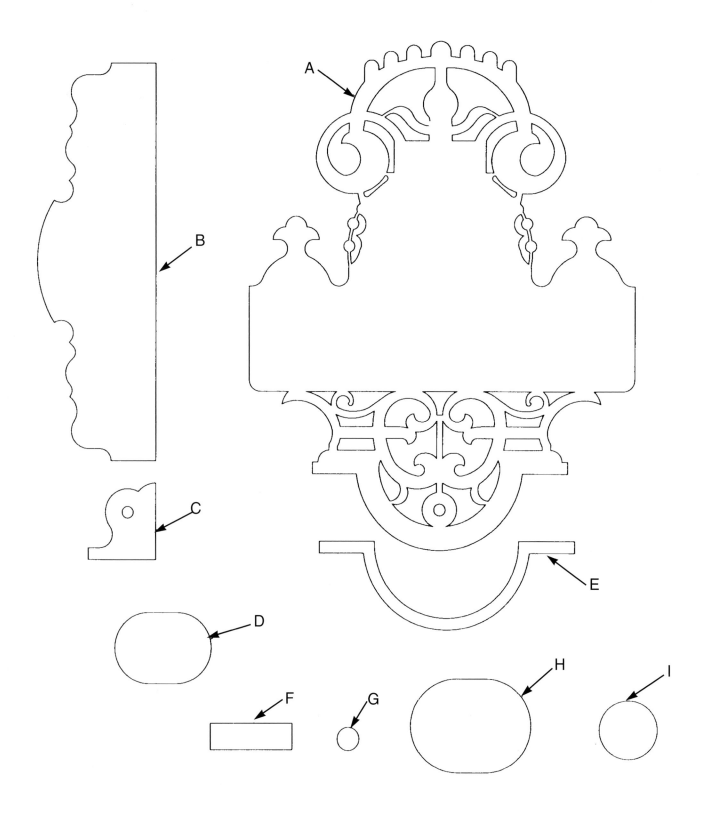

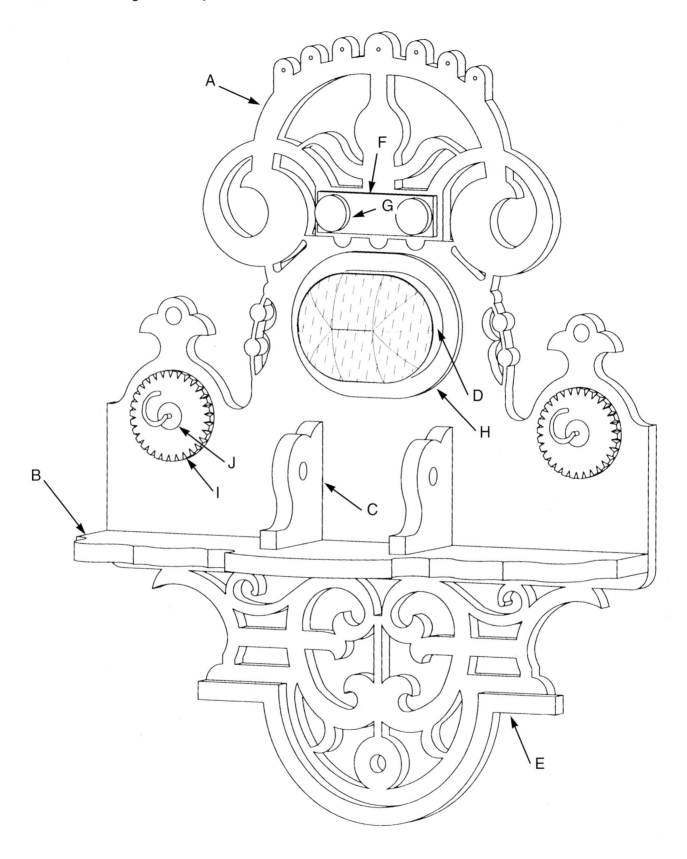

Plaid Pinwheel

Needle Keeper

The Scarf

Plaid Pinwheel

MATERIALS
Empty ribbon spool 3½" wide and ¾" deep
Two 5" circles of green fabric
11¾" x 1¾" strip of muslin
24" of green braid trim
Two 3⅛" circles of mat board
Stuffing
Tacky glue

DIRECTIONS
1. Fold under edges of circles of green fabric ¼" and hand-sew a gathering stitch close to edge. Place circle right side down. Place mat circles in center. Pull gathering thread tightly and tie in a knot.

2. With right sides facing, match short sides of muslin strip and sew ¼" seam. Sew gathering stitch around both long sides ¼" from edge. On one side, pull thread to make a 2½" opening. Pull over ribbon spool and glue. Stuff inside of spool firmly, causing the muslin to puff evenly around all sides. Pull other gathering thread tightly and glue down.

3. Center and glue circles of green fabric on each side of spool.

4. Glue green braid trim around green circle edge.

Needle Keeper

MATERIALS
⅛ yard of printed velvet; matching thread
⅛ yard of coordinating satin
7" x 4" piece of coordinating wool
12" of ¼" velvet ribbon
⅛ yard of heavy iron-on interfacing
Gold thread
Stuffing
Pinking shears

DIRECTIONS
1. Cut out all pattern pieces from page 30. Cut one 10½" x 1" strip of velvet.

2. With pinking shears, cut around edges of each wool piece. Using gold thread, sew a running row of lazy daisy stitches ¼" around the edge of each wool piece.

3. Place velvet pieces and satin pieces right side down on ironing board. Center interfacing pieces, bumpy side up, on each corresponding fabric piece. Fold fabric ¼" over interfacing and carefully iron around edges of all four pieces. Fold 10½" x 1" velvet piece ¼" on long side. Press. (This looks like a seam binding.)

4. To make the top, place one velvet fan-shaped piece and one satin fan-shaped piece wrong sides together. Slipstitch around three sides, using small, close-together stitches, leaving flat edge open. Set aside.

5. To make bottom, slipstitch 10½" x 1" velvet strip to bottom velvet fan-shaped piece. Slipstitch last satin fan-shaped piece to 10½" x 1" velvet strip, leaving straight edge open. Stuff firmly.

6. Layer needle holder pieces from bottom to top in the following order: large satin piece, small satin piece, large wool piece, and small wool piece. Sew ¼" on flat edge to secure. Position these on top of stuffed piece. Slide into opening left for stuffing and slipstitch closed.

7. Slipstitch top piece to the cushion at straight edge.

8. Cut velvet ribbon in half. Slipstitch half to center front top and half to center front bottom.

Sweet Rolls

Red Velvet Sweet Roll

MATERIALS
Empty 26-oz. Morton salt container
3¾" x 11¼" strip of print fabric
Two 6½" circles of red velvet
2¼" x 10¾" strip of iron-on interfacing
24" of blue braid trim
Two 3⅛" circles of mat board
Stuffing
Glue gun and glue sticks

DIRECTIONS
1. Cut a 2¼"-wide tube from empty salt container. Set aside.

2. Trim mat board circles to fit inside the tube. Cut a 1" circle in center of mat board circles.

3. Fold edges of one red velvet circle under ¼" and sew a gathering stitch close to edge. Slightly gather circle and stuff loosely. Place mat board circle inside cushion; gather tightly. Tie off. Through center hole, stuff firmly. Repeat for remaining red velvet circle. Set aside.

4. Wrap strip of interfacing around tube. Iron according to package instructions.

5. Fold short side of print fabric strip under ¼" and press. Wrap fabric around tube, leaving ¼" on each long edge. Glue seam. Fold ¼" edge to the inside of tube and glue. Let dry.

6. Push one velvet cushion in one end of tube. Hot-glue in place, leaving ¼" of cushion in tube. Repeat for other cushion.

7. Cut blue braid trim in half. Glue around each edge of tube.

Violets Sweet Roll

Violets Sweet Roll is made following the instructions for Red Velvet Sweet Roll. The finished design below is substituted for the piece of red velvet. The tube is smaller and covered with a strip of tapestry fabric. It is finished with dk. green cording and three shades of 4mm silk ribbon cascade down one side.

The design is stitched on cream Belfast linen 32 over 2 threads. The finished design size is 2¾" x 2¾".

FABRIC	DESIGN SIZES
Aida 11	4⅛" x 4"
Aida 14	3¼" x 3⅛"
Aida 18	2½" x 2½"
Hardanger 22	2" x 2"

Anchor		DMC (used for sample)	

Step 1: Cross-stitch (2 strands)

Anchor	Symbol	DMC	Name
386	+	746	Off White
886	╱	677	Old Gold-vy. lt.
891	B	676	Old Gold-lt.
901	H	680	Old Gold-dk.
297	Z	743	Yellow-med.
13	K	347	Salmon-vy. dk.
968	–	778	Antique Mauve-vy. lt.
969	G	316	Antique Mauve-med.
970	∴	315	Antique Mauve-vy. dk.
72	■	902	Garnet-vy. dk.
869	U	3743	Antique Violet-vy. lt.
870	E	3042	Antique Violet-lt.
871	✕	3041	Antique Violet-med.
872	W	3740	Antique Violet-dk.
859	△	3052	Green Gray-med.
846	R	3051	Green Gray-dk.
265	·	3348	Yellow Green-lt.
266	S	3347	Yellow Green-med.
268	N	3345	Hunter Green-dk.
862	●	934	Black Avocado Green
213	Y	369	Pistachio Green-vy. lt.
214	□	368	Pistachio Green-lt.
216	▲	367	Pistachio Green-dk.
370	○	434	Brown-lt.
371	M	433	Brown-med.

Stitch count: 45 x 44

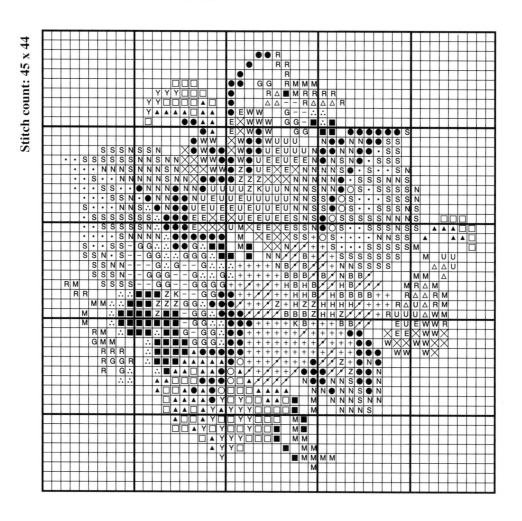

Roses Sweet Roll

Roses Sweet Roll is made following the instructions for Red Velvet Sweet Roll. The finished design below is substituted for the piece of red velvet. The tube is smaller and covered with a strip of cream Moiré fabric. It is finished with burgundy braid and four shades of 4mm silk ribbon tied in a bow.

Stitched on cream Belfast linen 32 over 2 threads. The finished design size is 2¾" x 2¾".

FABRIC	DESIGN SIZES
Aida 11	4⅛" x 4⅛"
Aida 14	3¼" x 3¼"
Aida 18	2½" x 2½"
Hardanger 22	2" x 2"

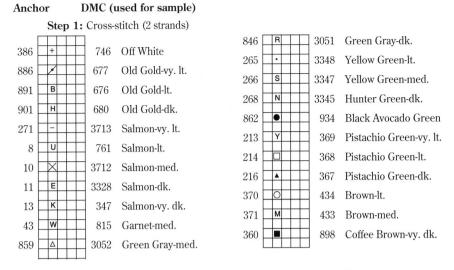

Anchor		DMC (used for sample)	
Step 1: Cross-stitch (2 strands)			
386	+	746	Off White
886	/	677	Old Gold-vy. lt.
891	B	676	Old Gold-lt.
901	H	680	Old Gold-dk.
271	-	3713	Salmon-vy. lt.
8	U	761	Salmon-lt.
10	X	3712	Salmon-med.
11	E	3328	Salmon-dk.
13	K	347	Salmon-vy. dk.
43	W	815	Garnet-med.
859	△	3052	Green Gray-med.
846	R	3051	Green Gray-dk.
265	·	3348	Yellow Green-lt.
266	S	3347	Yellow Green-med.
268	N	3345	Hunter Green-dk.
862	●	934	Black Avocado Green
213	Y	369	Pistachio Green-vy. lt.
214	□	368	Pistachio Green-lt.
216	▲	367	Pistachio Green-dk.
370	O	434	Brown-lt.
371	M	433	Brown-med.
360	■	898	Coffee Brown-vy. dk.

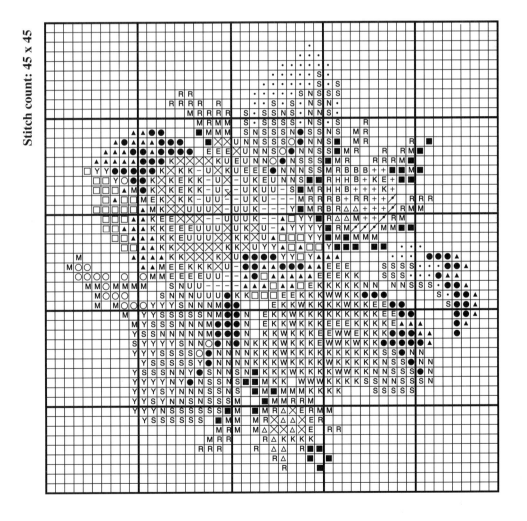

Stitch count: 45 x 45

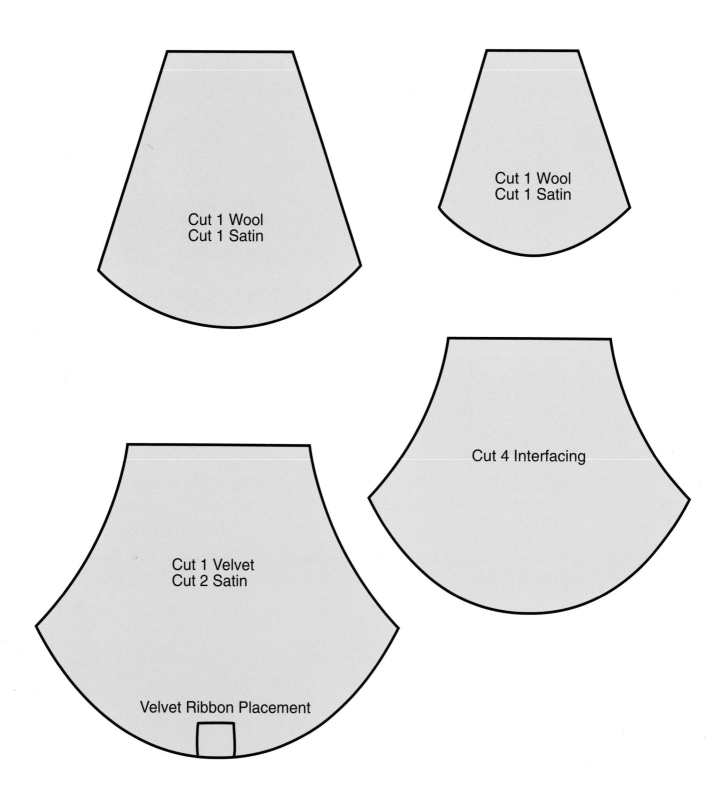

Cut 1 Wool
Cut 1 Satin

Cut 1 Wool
Cut 1 Satin

Cut 4 Interfacing

Cut 1 Velvet
Cut 2 Satin

Velvet Ribbon Placement

Charmed Blue Doily

MATERIALS

9" x 9" doily
6" x 12" piece of light blue fabric
7mm silk ribbon:
    3 yards of blush
    1 yard of white
    ½ yard of lt. blue
Silver charms:
    3 small hearts
    1 small rose
    3 cherubs
2 different shades of ⅝" blue wired
    ribbon: one 7" piece and one 7½"
      piece
Stuffing

DIRECTIONS

1. Cut the blue fabric in half so that you have two 6" squares. Sew right sides together, leaving one side open. Trim corners. Turn, stuff and stitch closed.

2. Center doily over top of pillow and sew around edges of pillow.

3. With the lt. blue silk ribbon, start at bottom center and weave through doily in a diamond pattern, finishing at your starting point. Cut and secure ribbon.

4. With the blush silk ribbon, weave through doily around the edge of pillow.

5. Tie 4 small bows with the blush ribbon and stitch one to each corner of pillow. Stitch the 3 hearts and 1 rose charm to the corners.

6. Make 4 rosettes with the white ribbon; see "Ribbon/Fabric Rosette" on page 15. Stitch or glue rosettes over bows.

7. With 7½" piece of wired ribbon, bring one end over to the other end, making a tube. Glue. Pinch and pleat one edge of the tube closed and glue. When dry, glue or stitch to center of pillow. Repeat with the 7" piece of ribbon. Attach to the top of other flower. Make a small bow with 8" of blush ribbon and glue to center of flower. Cascade the tails. Glue cherub charms in place with one in center and two holding bow tails.

Diamond Heart

MATERIALS

8" x 5" piece of cardboard
17" x 5" piece of satin
½ yard of 1"-wide old or new lace
Bits of old lace or tatting for top of heart
½ yard of 3 different colors of 4mm silk ribbon
Charms: tiny angel, filigree heart, bow
Piece of old jewelry or button to place over filigree heart
Stuffing
Tacky glue

DIRECTIONS

1. Cut 2 large cardboard hearts from patterns on page 35.

2. Cut a 12¼" x 2¾" strip of fabric. Cut a fabric heart that is ½" larger all around than the cardboard heart.

3. Wrap one of the cardboard hearts with the fabric heart. Glue edges to back.

4. To make stuffed heart, match short ends of the fabric strip and sew a ¼" seam. Sew a gathering stitch along both raw edges. Gather one edge so that it will fit around the other cardboard heart. Starting at top center, glue the gathered edge to underside of heart. Let dry completely.

5. Bring the other edge over top of heart and pull gathering thread, leaving about a 2" opening. Stuff firmly. Pull gathering thread to close and secure.

6. Glue old or new lace to underside of stuffed heart.

7. Glue or sew lace to top of heart.

8. Glue filigree heart over center of heart. Let dry.

9. Tie a small bow into the silk ribbons. Glue bow just above filigree heart.

10. Cascade silk ribbon tails. Thread one of the ribbons into an embroidery needle (size 3). Take a ⅛"-long stitch into the heart about ¾" away from the bow's knot. Backstitch next to the first stitch.

Take another ⅛"-long stitch about ¾" away from the previous cascaded stitch, and in the direction you wish to go. Backstitch next to this second stitch. Continue stitching and backstitching with each ribbon tail. Tuck ribbon ends under stuffed heart.

11. Glue stuffed heart to base heart.

12. Glue tiny angel, and tiny heart in place. Let dry.

Peach Heart

MATERIALS

8" x 4" piece of cardboard
8" x 12" piece of satin
Five 12" lengths of 4mm silk ribbon of five colors: pink, lavender, gray, green, rose
10" piece of braid
12" piece of gathered lace
1 ceramic heart
1 rosette
Stuffing
Glue

DIRECTIONS

1. Using patterns on page 35, cut one large heart and one small heart from cardboard.

2. From fabric, cut one large heart ½" larger than pattern. Glue large fabric heart to large cardboard heart, easing in fullness around the edges.

3. From fabric, cut one 11½" x 2½" strip. With right sides facing, sew ¼" seam across short edge, forming a tube. Glue ½" of tube around bottom of small cardboard heart with the seam at the dimple of the heart. Lightly stuff center and pleat tube opening. Stitch to secure pleats and pull fabric taut. Glue ceramic heart over opening.

4. Using all 12" lengths of silk ribbon, tie one bow. Position bow at top of ceramic heart and glue. Glue rosette at center of bow. Glue ends of ribbon under cushion, allowing for loops and fullness. Repeat with braid.

5. Glue gathered lace around edge of large heart base. Glue heart cushion to base.

Golden Oval

MATERIALS

4" x 5" piece of cardboard
6" x 9" piece of cream satin fabric
1 yard of 9mm white silk ribbon
30" each of 4mm silk ribbon: white and cream
7" braid
1 rosette
⅞" button
Stuffing
Glue gun and glue sticks

DIRECTIONS

1. Using patterns on page 35, cut large and small ovals from cardboard.

2. For pincushion base, cut one oval ½" larger than large oval pattern from cream satin fabric. Cover large oval cardboard piece with large oval fabric piece, hot-gluing around edge and easing in fullness. Set aside.

3. Cut a 2" x 8½" strip of fabric. Sew a ¼" seam across short end, forming a tube. Turn. Glue ½" of tube around bottom of small oval cardboard piece.

4. Hand-sew a gathering thread ¼" from fabric tube edge. Lightly stuff the box and pull thread. Ease gathers evenly and pull toward center tightly. The fabric should be taut. Stitch closed. Before cutting thread, sew button in center of cushion.

5. Flute 9mm ribbon along edge of pincushion base by gluing down one ribbon end to fabric, looping to desired length, and gluing in a series of even loops.

6. Glue cushion to base. Cut 4mm ribbon into 10" lengths. Tie a knot with all ribbons ½" from one end. Tie a bow 2" from knot. Fasten bow at bottom edge of button and tack ends of ribbon under the cushion; see photo. Ribbon will loop. Add braid and rosette near bow.

Patterns for Diamond Heart, Peach Heart, and Golden Oval

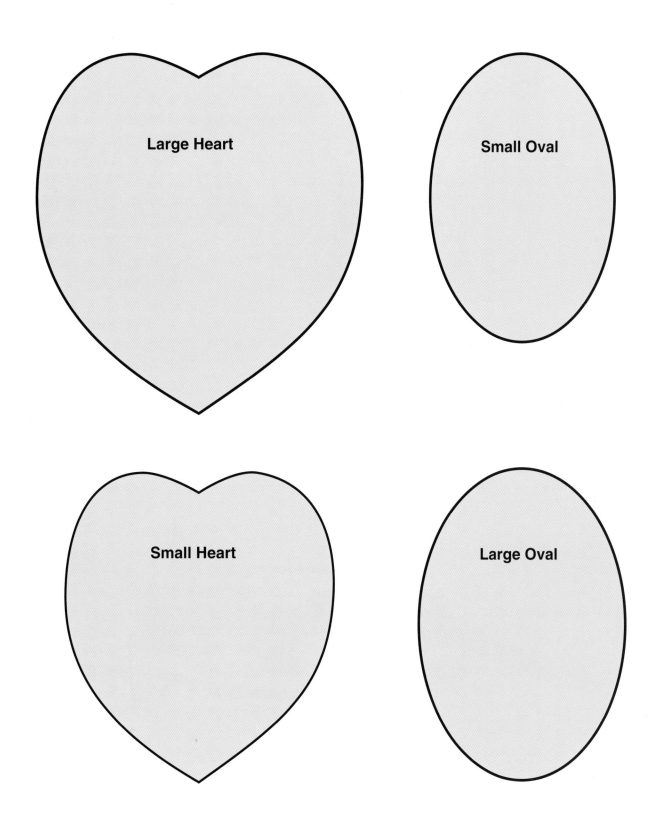

Large Heart

Small Oval

Small Heart

Large Oval

Eggs-actly What's Needed

Play tunes across the sea
Like 'Home Sweet Home'; above the foam
The Kegans call to me
As once again the Devon rain
Upsets their picnic tea.

NEAPOLITAN SANDWICHES

brown or white bread, thinly sliced
butter
fillings of different colours, eg tomato, pâté, watercress, egg

Butter two slices of bread on one side only, the remainder on both si
Place the unbuttered side of one slice on a breadboard or working-su
Spread the buttered side with one of the fillings, cover with a slice of t
and press it well down. Build up a 'loaf' alternating the fillings to give a
colourful effect. Cover the final layer of filling with the buttered side
remaining slice of bread that was buttered on only one side. Cut off t
and wrap the 'loaf' tightly in foil or clingfilm and put in the refrigerator
overnight with something heavy on top. Unwrap the 'loaf' and slice thinl
across the layers of fillings. Cut each slice into triangles to serve.

NB Make sure that the weight covers the 'loaf' evenly otherwise it will
difficult to slice and look messy.

Egg-sactly What's Needed

MATERIALS
4" Styrofoam egg
6" x 12" piece of pink satin
Six 2½" fabric circles in assorted colors
6" x 12" piece of fleece
¼ yard each of 7mm silk ribbon:
   six pastel shades
10" each of 4mm silk ribbon:
   nine pastel shades
½ yard of 4mm pink silk ribbon
Silk embroidery thread: five pink shades,
   two green shades
12" length of 1" variegated wired
   ribbon
9" length of ½" variegated wired
   ribbon
30 assorted seed beads and small
   pearls
6 rhinestones
3 small brass charms
Tacky glue

DIRECTIONS
1. Glue fleece around egg as smoothly as possible. Trim.

2. Fold satin in half, with right sides facing and short edges aligned, stitching ¼" seam. Press seam open. Turn and slip fabric tube over egg. Fold top edge down ¼" and stitch gathering thread around edge. Pull thread tightly to gather and secure. Glue gathered satin to egg. Repeat on bottom edge of egg.

3. Make six yo-yos with 2½" fabric circles; see "Fabric Yo-yo" on page 14. From 7mm silk ribbon, cut into six 9" lengths and make six rosettes; see "Ribbon /Fabric Rosette" on page 15. Cut 4mm silk ribbon into eighteen 5" lengths and make eighteen rosettes.

4. To place embroidered bullion petals, measure 1½" from top of egg. Lightly mark seven places at equal distance from each other around egg. Stitch bullion petals, alternating stitches with different shades of thread. With green silk embroidery thread, embroider leaves using lazy-daisy stitch. Thread needle with ½ yard of pink silk ribbon and cascade around bullions, twisting ribbon to give more curl. Stitch beads and pearls around roses; see photograph.

5. For placement of larger rosettes, measure 2½" from top center of egg. Lightly mark six places an equal distance from each other around egg. Glue rosettes in place. Glue three ⅛" rosettes, alternating colors, in an arch between larger rosettes. Glue yo-yos below arch. Glue rhinestones in yo-yo centers. Glue knot to center top of egg; see photo.

6. To make ribbon ruffles, fold 12" length of 1" wired ribbon with right sides facing and short edges aligned; glue or stitch small seam. Turn. Stitch gathering thread around one long edge of ribbon. Pull thread tightly to gather, leaving small center opening. Place ruffled ribbon circle on top of egg. Glue to egg without matting ruffles. Repeat, using 9" length of ½" wired ribbon.

7. Bend charms slightly so that they are flat against curved surface of egg; glue.

Ebony Half Egg

MATERIALS
Med. Styrofoam egg
4"-square Styrofoam block (2" high)
12" x 6" piece of black fabric
5½" circle of black fabric
1 yard of 1" gold braid
2 yards of 7mm lt. purple silk ribbon
4 yards of 7mm dk. purple silk ribbon
3 yards of 4mm green silk ribbon
10" of gold cord
3½" circle of heavy cardboard
Tacky glue

DIRECTIONS
1. Cut Styrofoam egg in half. From Styrofoam square, cut a 2¾" circle. Glue flat side of wider half of egg to flat side of circle, creating a dome. Let dry.

2. Using pattern A on page 91 (small leaf for Pineapple), cut six pieces from black fabric. Glue each piece around dome, matching seams.

3. Cut three 12" lengths from gold braid. Weave lt. purple silk ribbon through center of braid. Embellish along center of braid at regular intervals with silk ribbon, using dk. purple French knots and green lazy-daisy stitches; see page 15 for stitches (see photo). Starting at bottom edge of dome, glue one piece of gold braid, covering seam, up and over dome to opposite side bottom edge. Repeat for remaining pieces of gold braid.

4. Pulling snugly, gather 5½" fabric circle around cardboard circle and glue edges to wrong side of cardboard.

5. Flute dk. purple silk ribbon to wrong side of cardboard circle edge. Center and glue dome to wrong side of cardboard circle. Glue gold cord around bottom edge of dome.

6. Make roses from remaining lt. purple and dk. purple silk ribbon; see Ribbon Work on page 14. Glue to top of dome. Cascade from top with green silk ribbon.

Picture Perfect

MATERIALS
Oval decorative frame
Piece of lace or tatting
Scrap of material same size as frame
Stuffing

DIRECTIONS
1. Remove frame back. Place a large, even-shaped amount of stuffing over the top of cardboard piece included with the frame.

2. Cut fabric scrap 1" larger than cardboard piece. Cover stuffing with the fabric and glue edges to back.

3. Place lace or tatting across top end of cushion; see photo.

4. Glue cushion to inside of frame back and close.

Silver Treasures

MATERIALS
4"-square gift box (3¼" high)
4" square of heavy cardboard for lid top
4½" square of lightweight cardboard for lid center
3½" square of lightweight cardboard for underside of lid
16½" x 3¾" strip of lightweight cardboard for insert
3¾" square of lightweight cardboard for inside bottom
4" square of heavy cardboard for bottom
Gray silk fabric:
    6½" square for lid top

5½" square for lid center
34" x 4" strip for box sides
5½" square for bottom
17" x 2" strip for box top edge
Pink fabric:
    4½" square for underside of lid
    36" x 5½" strip for insert
    8" square for inside bottom
    2" x 16" strip for rose
18" of 2" gray gathered ribbon
60" of ½" tan gathered ribbon
4mm silk ribbon:
    15" piece of rose
    20" piece of gray

15" piece of beige
7mm silk ribbon:
    3" piece of gray
    20" piece of gray
    20" piece of pink
1 yard of pink cording
4" lace doily
Large and small heart charms
1 silver button
2 pearl beads
Fleece
Stuffing
Tacky glue

DIRECTIONS

1. Sew a gathering stitch ¼" from edge on both long sides of gray "box side" strip of fabric. Match short sides, right sides facing, and sew ¼" seam. Gather one edge, slip over box and glue to outside 1" from top edge. Gather remaining edge and glue to bottom edge of box.

2. Fold remaining gray strip lengthwise in half. Place over top edge of box and glue inside and out.

3. Cover cardboard square for bottom with 5" square of gray fabric and glue. Center and glue wrong side of bottom piece to bottom of the box. Glue gray gathered ribbon around box ⅛" down from top of box, covering raw edge of gray strip. (If desired, place small amount of stuffing under ribbon.)

4. For hinges, cut 3" length of 7mm gray silk ribbon in half. Glue end of one length 1" from corner on inside top edge of box; hang free edge of ribbon outside box. Repeat with other ribbon from opposite corner on same side of box.

5. Sew a gathering stitch on long sides of pink fabric strip for insert. Fold lightweight cardboard strip for insert to form a square and glue together. Gather fabric. Place fabric on inside of square. Glue overlapping fabric to outside of square top and bottom. Place this square inside box. Glue to secure.

6. Sew a gathering stitch around pink square for inside bottom. Gather slightly and stuff. Gather tightly around lightweight cardboard square for inside bottom. Center the cushion and glue inside bottom of box.

7. Glue fleece to heavy cardboard square for lid top. Trim. Center cardboard and fleece, fleece-side down, on wrong side of gray fabric square for lid top. Pulling snugly, wrap and glue edges to wrong side. Repeat with pieces for underside of lid.

8. Center lightweight cardboard square for lid center on wrong side of gray fabric square for lid center. Wrap edges and glue to wrong side of cardboard.

9. From tan gathered ribbon cut a 20" length, an 18" length, and a 16" length. Glue 20" length to edge of wrong side of lid center. Position 18" piece on top, ⅛" from outside edge of lid center. Glue. Glue 16" length ¼" from outside edge of lid center.

10. Place underside of lid right side down on box opening. Glue free edges of ribbon hinges to back. Center and glue right side of lid center and wrong side of underside of lid together. From pink cording, cut 14". Glue cording around edge of underside of lid. Close lid.

11. Embellish lid top. Make fabric rose from pink strip; see "Fabric Rose" on page 14. Make two rosettes from 7mm pink silk ribbon; see "Ribbon/Fabric Rosette" on page 15. From 4mm silk ribbon, make 4 rose-colored rosettes, 3 beige rosettes, and 2 gray rosettes. From tan gathered ribbon, make two gathered circles and sew a pearl bead in each center. Tack doily to upper left corner of lid top. Glue fabric rose to upper left corner. Glue ribbon rosettes around fabric rose as desired. Glue charms as desired. Fold 20" of gray silk ribbon and pink cording together in half to find the center and tie into a bow. Glue bow behind fabric rose. Cascade tails of ribbon and cording around two sides of lid top.

12. Center and glue lid top to lid center.

Antique Wooden Chest

MATERIALS

Parts A – Q as described on
  page 43
Wood recommendations: Dark California
  Walnut for all parts except parts F

and G which require a lt.-colored
  wood
9" circle of blue velvet for pincushion;
  matching thread
Stuffing

Wood glue
Drill and ⅜" bit
Clamp
Small screw
Table saw

Part	Description	Dimensions	Quantity
A	Posts	2" x ½" x ½"	8
B	Panels	4⅝" x 2" x 3/16"	4
C	Panels	3⅜" x 2" x 3/16"	2
D	Bottom Back Panel	5⅞" x 2" x 3/16"	1
E	Bottom and Middle Base	7" x 5¼" x ¼"	2
F	Designed Spire Dowels	⅜" diameter x 1¼"	8
G	Eyelets	⅜" diameter O.D. x ⅛" diamter I.D. x 3/16"	8
H	Feet	⅜" diameter x 1"	4
I	Spindle Holders	1/16" diameter x 1½"	8
J	Lid	5½" x 4" x 3/16"	1
K	Back Drawer Panel	5⅜" x 1⅝" x 3/16"	1
L	Side Drawer Panels	4⅝" x 2" x 3/16"	2
M	Front Drawer Panel	5⅜" x 2" x ¼"	1
N	Drawer Bottom	5⅜" x 4½" x 3/16"	1
O	Drawer Handle	⅜" diameter x ¾"	1
P	Cushion Backing	1½" diameter x ¼"	1
Q	Panel Supports	¼" x ¼" x 3½"	4

DIRECTIONS

1. Cut wood parts on table saw to indicated dimensions.

2. On parts A, add 3/16" dado cuts for side panels off center toward the outside of box. Drill ⅜"-diameter holes on both ends for dowel pins.

3. Either turn parts F, H, and O on a lathe or purchase from a crafts store. These dowels are used to join E together.

4. Rabbet ends of K and M to fit L. Add 3/16" dado cut on K, M, and L to fit N.

5. Sew a ¼" gathering stitch around edge of velvet circle. Pull threads until velvet cups. Stuff firmly. Pull threads tightly around P and secure. Screw P onto J from back.

6. Drill ⅜" holes at corners of J and round off resulting sharp edges to fit around dowels (F).

7. Assemble, using wood glue between all mating parts; clamp.

8. Put a slight angle on the rear sides of the drawer so that it slides in easily without catching.

9. Use suitable steel pins or ⅛"-diameter dowel pins for part I. Install them spaced for thread spools. Space eyelets (G) to correspond with pins (I).

Antique Wooden Chest Assembly

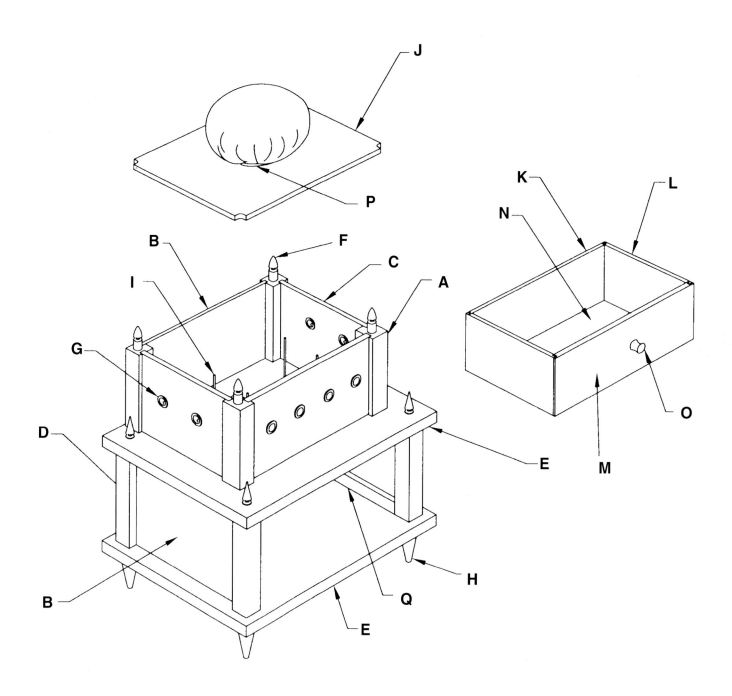

44

Patterns for Verdant Oval on page 47

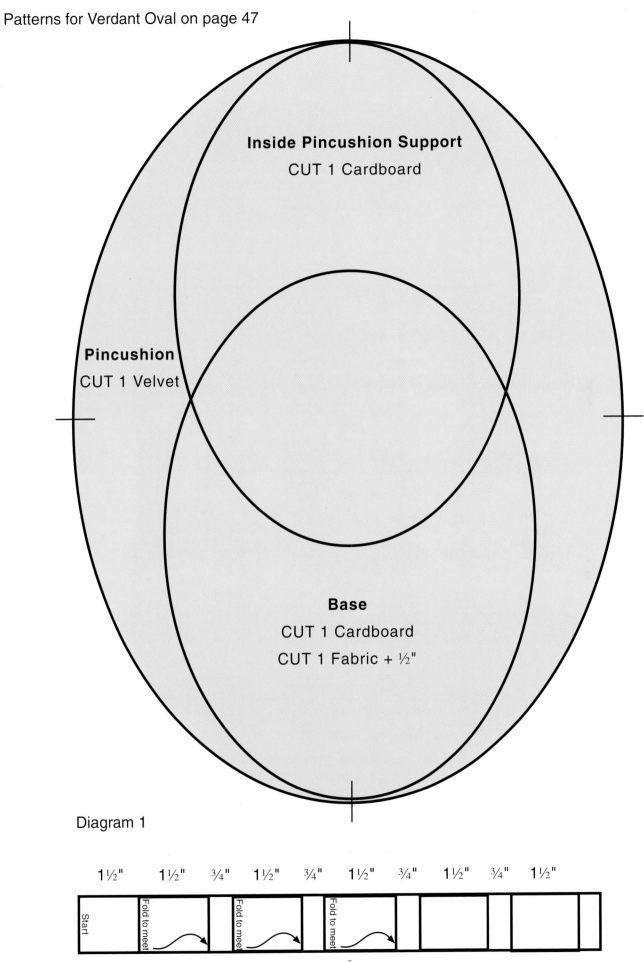

Inside Pincushion Support

CUT 1 Cardboard

Pincushion

CUT 1 Velvet

Base

CUT 1 Cardboard

CUT 1 Fabric + ½"

Diagram 1

| 1½" | 1½" | ¾" | 1½" | ¾" | 1½" | ¾" | 1½" | ¾" | 1½" |

Start | Fold to meet | | Fold to meet | | Fold to meet | | | | |

Verdant Oval

MATERIALS

3" x 16" piece of lightweight, bendable cardboard
6" x 9" piece of heavyweight cardboard
16" x 7" piece of velvet
17" x 2½" piece of fabric for lining side
1 yard of narrow trim
¾ yard of narrow lace
1½ yards of 1½" wired ribbon
Brass heart and bow charms
Stuffing

DIRECTIONS

1. Cut two 1½" x 16" strips of bendable cardboard. Cover one of these strips with fabric. Cut one each of the oval shapes from the heavyweight cardboard using oval patterns on page 45.

2. Cut one pincushion oval from velvet. Cut one oval from velvet that is ½" larger than the base cardboard piece. Cover the base cardboard piece with this piece of velvet.

3. Roll the uncovered strip of cardboard onto a dowel so that cardboard curves. Using the uncovered strip of cardboard, overlap cardboard 1⅜" and glue. Shape strip around inside cushion support oval. Mark strip to indicate the sides and the center front and back in accordance with oval shape.

4. Glue velvet pincushion piece to oval-shaped cardboard, matching up side markings, and center front and back markings. Overlap the velvet ½" onto the upper edge of the oval-shaped cardboard. Glue the velvet all around oval strip, finger-easing the fabric as you glue.

5. Stuff velvet as firm as possible. Extend stuffing into oval-shaped cardboard. Push the inside cushion support cardboard piece into the oval-shaped cardboard strip so that the velvet has a firm bubble look. The oval cardboard can be pushed more than halfway into the oval-shaped strip. Hold the inside pincushion support piece firmly in place as you hot-glue all around outer edges where it meets the oval-shaped strip. Glue half of the oval, let glue dry, then glue the remaining half. (This inside support piece keeps the stuffing in place, and also keeps the pincushion from being too large.) You may need to adjust some of the puckers on the pincushion. Unpeel the glue, reglue, and reapply fabric until the pincushion has the shape desired.

6. Glue lace trim to the inside top edge of the fabric-covered strip. Roll cardboard onto dowel so that it curves. Glue the inside top edge of this outer strip to the pincushion, matching up the bottom

edges of each strip. You will notice that the strip does not fit snugly around the bottom edge. Ignore the misfit, but keep the edges even. Continue to glue all around, overlapping the ends.

7. Mark ribbon with a disappearing pen, as shown on Diagram 1 on page 45, until you have 23 spaces of 1½" each and 22 spaces of ¾" each. On the first mark, fold ribbon .Then fold to meet second mark. Pin down center. Fold again at the next mark; then fold to meet 4th mark. Pin down center. Continue to fold the entire length of ribbon. When all folding is complete, stitch ribbon down center for the entire length of ribbon, removing pins as you go.

8. Glue folded ribbon (at center stitching only) over fabric-covered strip. Glue narrow trim over stitching. Also glue narrow trim over lace. Fold each corner of the folded ribbon down to form a series of triangles.

9. Glue velvet base to pincushion bottom.

10. Stitch brass charms to center front or as desired.

Petite Package

MATERIALS

Three different 5" x 10" fabric pieces
24" of ⅛" decorative ribbon
18" of 1" variegated wired ribbon in 2 shades
2 wired leaves
Stuffing
Tacky glue

DIRECTIONS

1. Cut each fabric piece in half and sew right sides together, leaving an opening for stuffing. Turn and stuff each pillow.

2. Stack pillows on top of each other and tie the ribbon around them "present" style. Secure with glue.

3. To make pansy, cut one 6" and two 3" strips of one shade of wired ribbon and two 3" strips of the other shade. Gather one wired edge of each ribbon and glue, holding until glue sets. When dry, glue the three petals of the same shade together in a circle. Glue the other two petals on top. Glue the two wired leaves in between. Make a small ball from one of the ribbons and glue in center. Glue to top of pillows.

Pin Puff

MATERIALS

¼ yard of 45" gray fabric; matching thread

Small pieces of pink, plum, and dk. green fabrics; matching thread

⅝ yard of 4mm gray silk ribbon

⅝ yard of 4mm dk. green silk ribbon

¼ yard of ⅛" cranberry grosgrain ribbon

¼ yard of fleece

¼ yard of fusible interfacing

Stuffing

Dressmaker's pen

Tracing paper for patterns

DIRECTIONS

Prepare fabric

1. From pattern on page 49, make pattern for flower petals, flower background, leaf and 6½" circle. To make circle pattern, tie string around pencil; make knot 3¼" from pencil. Place knot on center of paper, hold with thumb and rotate pencil in circle around knot. Correct any irregularities.

2. From gray fabric, cut three circles like pattern for cushion and one 2" x 72" strip for shirring, piecing as needed.

3. From plum fabric, add ¼" seam allowance and cut two background pieces. Also cut three 2" x 1½" pieces for raised flower.

4. From pink fabric, add ¼" seam allowance and cut two sets of petal pieces (ten petals). Also cut one ⅜" x 1½" piece for raised flower bud.

5. From dk. green fabric, add ¼" seam allowance and cut one leaf. Also cut one 1" x 2" bias piece for raised leaf and one ½" x 8½" bias strip for stems.

6. From interfacing and from fleece, cut

one 6½" circle. Also from fleece, without adding seam allowances, cut two background pieces and one leaf.

Appliqué top

1. Mark placement for design on right side of one gray circle with dressmaker's pen; see Diagram 1 below.

2. Fold long edges of ½" x 8½" stem piece under ⅛"; press. From stem piece, cut a 4½" length, a 3" length and two 1" lengths. Knot one end of 3" length.

3. Fold three plum petal pieces in half to measure 2" x ¾". Make three fabric petals. Tack petals in place.

4. Appliqué stems, placing knot of 3" length over raw ends of plum petals.

5. Fold long edges of green piece for raised leaf under ¼". Make a fabric leaf. Tack raw edges behind leaf and tack in place.

6. Fold long edges of pink bud piece under ⅛". Tie piece into knot. Tucking raw ends underneath, tack bud in place.

7. Match fleece leaf to wrong side of dk.

green leaf. Turning edges under ¼", appliqué leaf.

8. Match fleece background pieces to wrong side of plum background pieces. Turning edges under ¼", appliqué pieces.

9. Turning edges under ¼", appliqué pink petal pieces of flower over left plum background piece. Repeat for right flower.

10. Place one fleece circle between wrong sides of gray fabric circle with appliqué and one plain gray fabric circle. Stitch around circle ⅛" from edges. Fold circle into quarters and mark.

11. With single strand of gray thread, quilt around outlines of flowers, stems and leaves. Also quilt vein in appliquéd leaf.

Construct cushion

1. With right sides of shirring strip together, stitch ¼" seam in 2" ends. Fold into quarters and mark both edges. Sew a gathering stitch ⅛" and ¼" on both long edges. Gather one edge only to fit cir-

cumference of circle.

2. Matching quarter marks and raw edges, right side of appliquéd circle to right side of shirring, stitch ¼" seam around circle.

3. Match interfacing circle to wrong side of remaining gray fabric and fuse according to manufacturer's instructions. Fold circle into quarters and mark.

4. Gather remaining edge of shirring to fit circumference of circle. Matching quarter marks and raw edges, right side of gray fabric circle with interfacing to right side of shirring, stitch ¼" seam around circle, leaving 3" opening. Turn.

5. Stuff firmly. Slipstitch opening closed.

6. Cut grosgrain ribbon into three equal lengths. Tie each piece into one knot. Trim excess ribbon. Tuck ends underneath and tack into place.

7. Handling both silk ribbons as one, tie into 2"-wide bow. Tack bow to cushion among grosgrain knots. Tie knots in ribbon ends at random lengths.

Flower and Leaf Pattern

Diagram 1

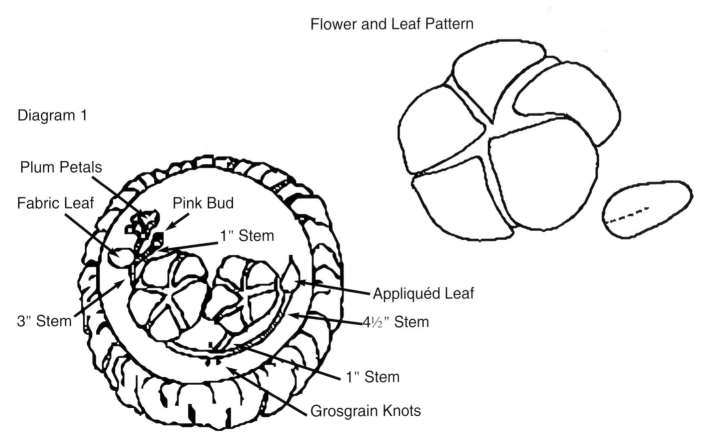

Plum Petals

Fabric Leaf

Pink Bud

1" Stem

3" Stem

Appliquéd Leaf

4½" Stem

1" Stem

Grosgrain Knots

Pleated Paisley

MATERIALS
2" of 3" postal tube
Two 3" circles of cardboard
2½" circle of cardboard
8½" x 1¾" strip of cardstock paper
10" circle and 5" circle of fabric
5" circle and 3¾" circle of contrasting fabric for lining
9½" x 3" strip of contrasting fabric for lining
2" x 12" strip of fleece
Three 3" circles of fleece
Tacky glue

DIRECTIONS
1. Form box by gluing one 3" circle of cardboard to bottom of tube.

2. Glue strip of fleece around the outside of box and glue one circle of fleece to outside bottom of box.

3. Cover the other 3" cardboard circle with a 3" fleece circle and glue. This will be the lid.

4. Run a gathering stitch ¼" from edge of 10" circle of fabric. Lay box on top of the wrong side of this fabric and pull gathering thread so that the box fits snugly inside. Glue edges of fabric evenly to inside of box.

5. Cover lid with fabric by gluing edges underneath. Pull snugly so that fabric is tight. Cover the 2½" circle with lining fabric and glue edges under, making sure that the fabric lies smoothly. Center the smaller circle on bottom of lid and glue.

6. On one long side of lining strip, press ⅜" under. Slide cardstock paper strip under the hem and lightly glue. Hold strip in a circle with hem side out and on top. Fit lining into box and glue, covering all raw edges of fabric.

7. With the last circle of lining and fleece, form a cushion to fill the bottom of the box. Glue the cushion to inside bottom of box, making sure that all raw edges are turned under and secured.

Oriental Pleasure

MATERIALS

2" Styrofoam ball
6¼" square piece of print fabric
5½" circle of solid fabric
Large and small bead for top
⅛ cup of rice

DIRECTIONS

1. Turn edges of circle under ¼". Sew a gathering stitch ⅛" from edge. Place Styrofoam ball in center, pull gathering thread tight and tie ends together.

2. Press all four sides of square under ¼". Fold at corner 1 matching wrong sides of A and B; see Diagram 1. Slipstitch 2½" from corner toward center; see Diagram 2. Repeat for corners 2, 3, and 4 matching corresponding sides.

3. Using a funnel, pour rice through ½"

opening in center. Place covered Styrofoam ball on center of opening (gathered side down). Test to be sure corner points reach top of ball (if not, roll ball on flat surface to compact it).

Diagram 1

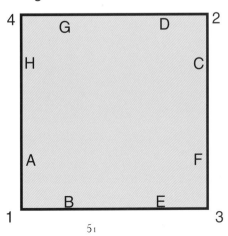

4. Slipstitch to opening. Pull four corners up around ball and secure. Do not cut thread. Attach beads to top.

Diagram 2

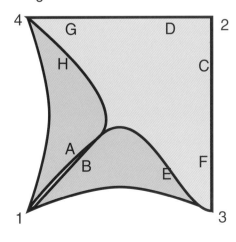

Victorian Cone-otations

MATERIALS (for cone with tassel)

Small empty thread cone
12" square of dusty rose Moiré Benzaline fabric
48" of 2" ecru cotton lace
24" of dusty rose/pink silk ribbon garland
1 yard of ⅛" pink silk ribbon
½ yard of ⅛" lt. green silk ribbon
144 AB crystal seed beads
Purchased 3" dusty rose tassel
Stuffing
Tacky glue

DIRECTIONS

1. Embroider design onto dusty rose fabric; see Diagram 1. (Beads are stitched onto fabric between cascading stitches as a final touch.)

2. Apply glue to outside top edge, outside bottom edge and in a ¼" strip from top to bottom of cone. Place cone on wrong side of fabric; see Diagram 2.

3. Roll fabric onto cone until edges meet. Secure edges with glue. Trim off excess fabric, allowing ½" at top and bottom. Glue inside cone.

4. Trace top circle of cone, adding ¼", and cut from dusty rose fabric.

5. To make cushion, stuff cone firmly and cover top of cone with dusty rose fabric circle. Glue ¼" edge to inside of cone, easing around stuffing.

6. Stitch a ¾" gathering thread in ecru cotton lace. Gather lace to measure 1 yard. Glue 24" of lace to raw seam line on back of cone from top to bottom. Trim off excess and tuck bottom end inside cone. Glue silk garland on gathered line of lace from top to bottom of cone. Trim and tuck bottom end inside cone.

7. Glue gathered line of remaining lace to top edge of cone with ¾" showing above the cone edge. Turn raw edges under and glue. Glue silk garland on gathered line of lace.

8. Glue silk garland on top of cushion just inside lace edging.

9. With remaining beads, string three uneven loops and glue inside bottom of cone. Glue tassel inside bottom of cone.

Diagram 1

▨	Cascade Stitch
▨	Ribbon Rosette
▨	Lazy-Daisy Stitch
▨	Lazy-Daisy Stitch
▨	Fern Stitch

Diagram 2

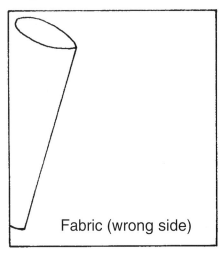

Fabric (wrong side)

Variations

The other cones pictured are patterned after this cone. One is covered with lace fabric and has a handle stemming from the cushion, and a plastic cherub adorns its face. Both are trimmed with gathered lace and silk ribbon garland. Knotted silk ribbon streamers fall from the small end.

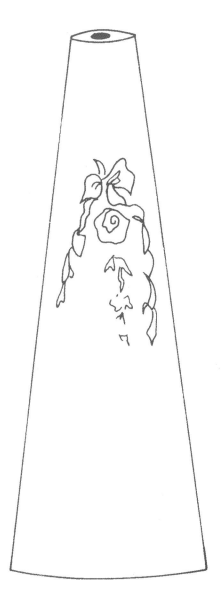

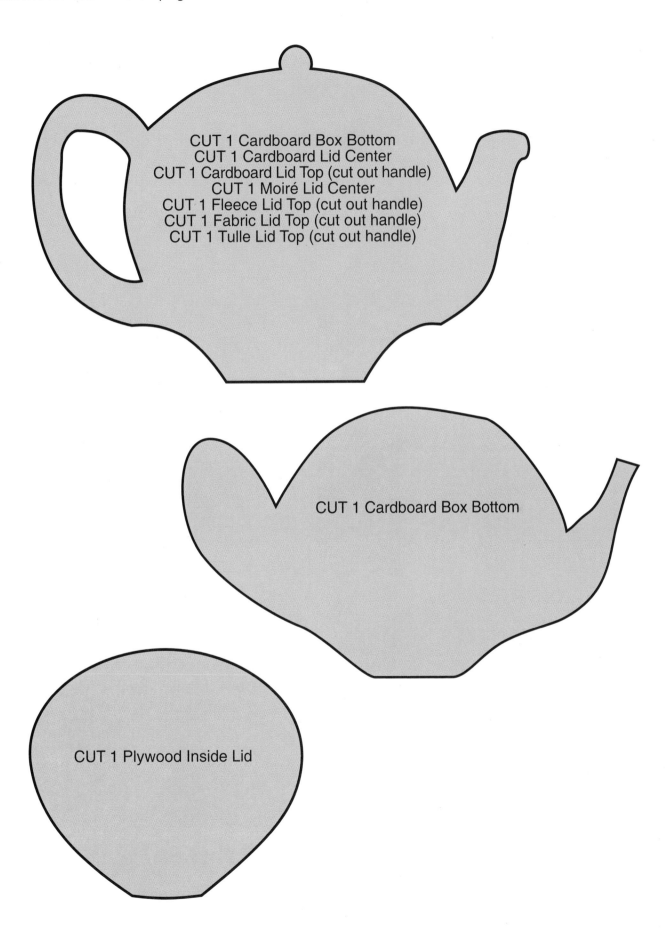

CUT 1 Cardboard Box Bottom
CUT 1 Cardboard Lid Center
CUT 1 Cardboard Lid Top (cut out handle)
CUT 1 Moiré Lid Center
CUT 1 Fleece Lid Top (cut out handle)
CUT 1 Fabric Lid Top (cut out handle)
CUT 1 Tulle Lid Top (cut out handle)

CUT 1 Cardboard Box Bottom

CUT 1 Plywood Inside Lid

A Recipe For the Ages

GRANDMOTHER HARRIET'S MOLASSES COOKIES

(makes about 7 dozen)
¾ cup shortening
1 cup molasses, preferably dark
1 cup brown sugar
1 cup sour milk (add 2 table-spoons vinegar to make sour)
6 cups flour
½ teaspoon salt (less is okay)
2 teaspoons ginger
4 teaspoons baking soda
1 tablespoon lemon extract
1 teaspoon cinnamon
½ teaspoon cloves

Mix shortening, molasses and sugar until smooth. Add sour milk. Sift flour with salt, ginger, baking soda, cinnamon and cloves. Add to molasses mixture. Add lemon extract. Mix until it becomes a smooth, stiff dough and chill overnight or until firm. Roll out on floured surface to a thickness of ⅓ inch. (May be rolled thinner for crisper cookies.) Cut into shapes. Place on greased baking sheet and bake in 350-degree oven 8 to 10 minutes. Decorate when cool.

(allowing ½" for seam), 1 doubled width of box side, and 1 base (allowing ½" for seam). From tulle, cut 1 lid top (allowing ½" for seam).

2. Glue fleece to lid top. Center lid top, fleece side down, on wrong side of lid top fabric. Pulling snugly, wrap and glue edges to wrong side. Place two ½"-wide strips of scrap mint green fabric on top of lid; see photo on page 56. Stretch tulle over lid top; wrap and glue edges on back.

3. Cover lid center with Moiré, overlapping onto the wrong side an extra 1½" where handle shows through. Glue braid around wrong side edge from bottom of handle to bottom of spout. Glue lavender crochet trim along bottom of lid center.

4. Cover plywood piece with Moiré and glue to fabric side of lid center. Glue lid top and lid center together wrong sides facing.

5. Cover box bottom with fleece and glue. Repeat with with Moiré, overlapping edges and gluing to wrong side.

6. Fold box side fabric in half lengthwise and laminate onto both sides of box side cardboard.

7. To shape, place dowel at one end of

box side and roll cardboard tightly around dowel. Place box side around box bottom and begin gluing outer edges of box bottom to inner edge of box side, small sections at a time. Glue together where ends meet.

8. Cover base with fabric, overlapping and gluing to wrong side. Glue scalloped lace around edge of wrong side of base. Glue base onto box bottom, wrong sides together.

9. To embellish lid top, make seven ¼" rosettes: 3 lavender and 2 each of lt. blue and lt. pink ribbon; see "Ribbon/Fabric Rosette" on page 15. Arrange rosettes on lid top along top edge of green fabric. Stitch ricrac along other edges of green fabric. Make a small bow with 18" of lavender ribbon and cascade ribbon over lid top. Repeat with 18" of lt. green ribbon, omitting bow. Attach pearls among rosettes and seed beads along ribbon.

10. With 12" lengths of pink, lavender, and blue ribbon, combine together and make bow. Knot ends. Glue cover seam on box side. Make a fabric rose from lavender tricot and 2 green ribbon leaves. Glue onto center of bow.

MATERIALS
Sugar bowl and saucer
4" Styrofoam ball
6" circle of pink satin
6" circle of lace fabric
12" piece of ½" gathered lace
Kitchen knife
Tacky glue

DIRECTIONS
1. Measure diameter inside pattern of your sugar bowl. With kitchen knife, cut

one side off Styrofoam ball to fit inside the pattern.

2. Sew a gathering stitch ¼" around satin circle. Cover rounded side of Styrofoam and pull threads tightly. Tie off.

3. Weave a gathering stitch through lace fabric. Place over satin-covered Styrofoam. Pull threads tightly and tie off.

4. Glue gathered edge of lace, 3" to 4" at a time, ¼" inside outer edge on flat side of Styrofoam.

5. Glue around edge of flat side of "cushion." Place inside pattern of sugar bowl and secure.

NOTE: If desired, stuffing may be substituted for the Styrofoam ball. Stuff satin circle firmly.

Cherubs

MATERIALS
3½" x 9" paper maché box
Four 3" terra cotta cherubs
Acrylic paints: med. flesh, off-white
Brass-finish corners and cherub charm
E-6000 adhesive

DIRECTIONS
1. Paint box with a base coat of med. flesh. Let dry.

2. Wash box with off-white paint by thinning paint with water and applying mixture in random directions. Let dry.

3. Using adhesive, glue brass corners to front lower corners of box. Center cherub charm on front of box and glue.

4. On underside of the box, place small amount of adhesive on each corner.

5. Position terra cotta cherubs in a square. Set box bottom on top of cherubs so that each corner of the box is supported by the head of one cherub; see photo.

58

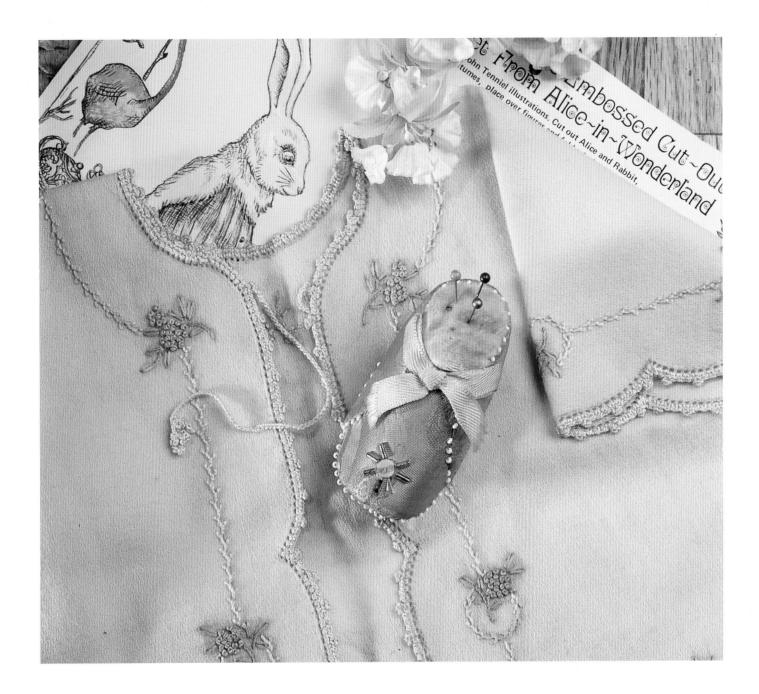

Antique Bootie

MATERIALS
6"-square piece of fabric
2"-square piece of velvet
8" of ¼" ribbon
Lightweight cardboard
1 package of small seed beads
Assorted beads for toe design
Stuffing
Adhesive spray

DIRECTIONS
1. Trace pattern pieces from page 60 onto lightweight cardboard. Working with one piece at a time, spray with adhesive and lay onto wrong side of fabric. Cut out fabric, leaving ¼" edges. Fold edges over and glue.

2. Place heel and toe around bottom sole in shape of a shoe (back overlapping the front). Once the top pieces match, glue them together and let dry. Lay the bottom into place and hand-sew to the top pieces.

3. Hand-stitch seed beads ⅛" apart around the bottom and front seams.

4. Stuff shoe tightly.

5. Cut a 1½" circle from velvet. Tuck into top of shoe and stitch in place. Add the seed beads around top seam.

6. Make a bow with ribbon and glue into place at top center of shoe.

7. Add assorted beads to toe as desired.

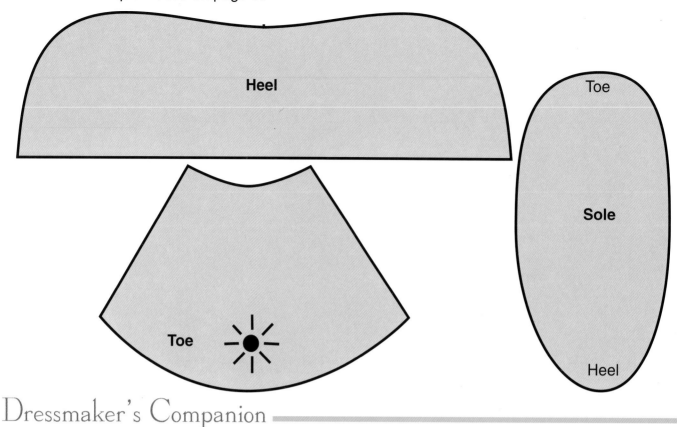

Heel

Toe

Sole

Toe

Heel

Dressmaker's Companion

MATERIALS
5" x 10" piece of muslin
5 printed handkerchiefs (or 10" squares of hemmed fabric)
6" plastic doll
Miniature gold bells with bow
String
Straight pins
Stuffing

DIRECTIONS
1. With right sides facing, fold muslin, matching short edges. Stitch long edge, making a tube. Gather one short edge tightly and secure. Turn. Gather other edge loosely. Stuff firmly. Tighten gathering thread and secure. Remove legs from doll and stitch doll torso to one of the gathered edges.

2. To make hat, fold one handkerchief in half diagonally; see Diagram 1. Continue folding into fourths; see Diagram 2A. Center handkerchief on doll forehead with tip of V pointing up; see Diagram 2B. Cross handkerchief in back of head and pin. Fold ends, accordion style, into side of doll's head, pinning each fold; see Diagram 3.

3. Fold second handkerchief in half diagonally; see Diagram 1. Continue folding; see Diagram 4A & 4B. Center handkerchief on doll chest with tip of V pointing down. Wrap under arms and cross in back. Pin. Bring ends over shoulders and cross in front. Pin.

4. Lay third handkerchief flat, wrong side up. Center pincushion on handkerchief. Draw fabric around pincushion and secure with thread at the bodice. Arrange points like flower petals. Repeat with remaining handkerchiefs, offsetting points to create a full look. Wrap string around handkerchiefs at doll's waist.

5. Tack miniature bells at waist.

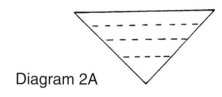

Diagram 2A

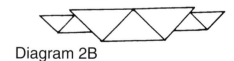

Diagram 2B

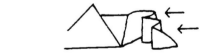

Diagram 3

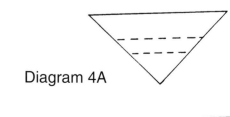

Diagram 4A

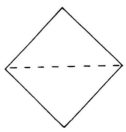

Diagram 1

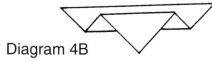

Diagram 4B

Boxful of Buds

MATERIALS
4"-square wooden frame
4"-square piece of cardboard
9"-square turquoise brocade fabric;
    matching thread
3"-square turquoise brocade fabric
Four 1½" circles of dusty rose Moiré
    fabric
1 yard of 4mm lt. green silk ribbon
1 yard of 4mm rose silk ribbon
14" silk ribbon garland
5 lt. pink rosettes
5 pink rosebuds
6 plastic leaves
4 small covered buttons for legs
Stuffing
Tacky glue

DIRECTIONS
1. Fern-stitch a horseshoe pattern on 3" square of fabric with lt. green silk ribbon and make French knots around pattern with rose silk ribbon; see page 14 for stitches. See Diagram 1 for placement of stitches and ribbon leaves, rosettes and buds; see Ribbon Work on pages 14–15. Glue piece of cardboard to one side of frame. Apply glue to outside of cardboard. Center cardboard side of frame onto wrong side of 9" fabric square.

2. Slash each corner of fabric to bottom corner of glued-down fabric; see Diagram 2. Bring each section up and around wooden frame, gluing small sections at a time to frame. Center and glue fabric inside frame. Trim off excess material.

3. Firmly stuff center of frame. Cover with embroidered 3" square of fabric, gluing raw edges into hole, making a cushion.

4. Glue silk ribbon garland around edge of cushion and on each corner, covering raw edges; see Diagram 1. Glue plastic leaves at each cushion corner. Set aside.

5. Hand-stitch a gathering thread around one 1½" dusty rose circle. Place a ball of stuffing in center of circle and gather tightly, making a pouf; see Diagram 3. Tie off. Repeat for remaining circles.

6. Using contrasting color of thread, draw a doubled thread through center of pouf to top center. Wrap thread around to bottom center and draw tightly up to top center. Wrap thread around three more sections, always stitching through center. Tie off. The pouf will be quartered when finished; see Diagram 4. Stitch or glue a rhinestone to top center of pouf. Repeat for remaining poufs.

7. Glue pouf to each top corner of box.

8. Glue one covered button to each bottom corner.

Diagram 1

	Fern Stitch		French Knot
	Ribbon Leaf		Ribbon Rosette
	Ribbon Bud		

Diagram 2

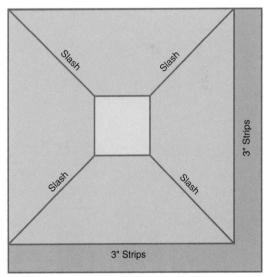

Diagram 3

Diagram 4

Purple Hearts

Violets

MATERIALS
10" square of heavyweight cardboard
18" x 1¼" strip of lightweight cardboard
½ yard of print velvet fabric
20" x 2" strip of print velvet fabric
4" square of contrasting silk fabric
1 yard of 9mm lt.-colored silk ribbon
½ yard of 9mm dk.-colored silk ribbon
½ yard of metallic cord
½ yard of metallic braid
8" of 2" scalloped metallic lace
1 pkg of small glass beads
1 pkg of small bugle beads
6 large flower-shaped beads
Stuffing
Tacky glue

DIRECTIONS
1. Using pattern on page 67, cut one heart from 10" cardboard square for base. Cut two velvet hearts adding ¾" around. Cover base with one velvet heart, overlapping and gluing edges to wrong side. Cover cardboard strip with velvet strip, overlapping and gluing to wrong side. Shape cardboard strip around covered base for sides. Glue outer edge of base to inner, bottom edge of strip, small sections at a time. Start and end the strip at the dimple at the top of the heart.

2. Glue the braid at the bottom edge of heart where base and sides meet, covering the raw edges. Glue a piece of braid to cover the seam at the dimple of the heart.

3. Stuff box firmly. At the point of the heart, begin gluing the right side edge of remaining velvet heart along the inside-edge of side of the heart, ⅜" from the top. Continue gluing, easing fullness.

4. Glue cording around the inside of the heart side to cover any glue or flaws.

5. For decorations, make small round pincushions from the following circles:

one 4" circle of silk fabric
two 1½" circles of velvet
two 1¼" circles of velvet
one 1" circle of velvet
Hand-gather circles ⅛" from edge. Stuff "cushion", packing lightly.

6. Stitch bugle beads to center in a sunburst pattern on the silk cushion. Use only one bugle bead on the smaller cushions to indicate the centers.

7. Gather seven 3"-3½" lengths of silk ribbon into rosettes, making 5 lt.-colored rosettes and 3 dk.-colored rosettes; see Ribbon Work on page 15. Stitch 3-5 small glass beads in the center of the rosettes to form stamens.

8. Gather scalloped lace into a circle.

9. Glue flowers on top of heart in the following order:
A- scalloped lace circle
B- silk pincushion
C- 1½" cushions
D- 1¼" cushions
E- 1" cushions
F- rosettes
G- flower beads
See Diagram 1 on page 67 for placement.

Lavender

MATERIALS
10" square of heavyweight cardboard
6" x 18" piece of purple velour or velvet fabric
6" x 6" piece of aqua velour or velvet fabric
12" x 12" piece of fleece
½ yard of antiqued silver braid trim
48" of 9mm silk ribbon for rosettes
Beads for centering on rosettes
200 turquoise Rocaille beads
Eight ⅛" iris beads
Stuffing
Tacky glue

DIRECTIONS
1. Cut one heart from pattern on page 67 using cardboard square. Apply glue to outer ¼" edge of cardboard heart. Press a layer of fleece onto glue. Let dry and trim around heart. Glue a second layer of fleece on top of first. Let dry and trim.

2. Cut heart shape from purple fabric, allowing ⅜" all around pattern. Place over top of batting and glue to underside of heart.

3. Cut another heart from purple fabric, this time cutting exact pattern. Glue this piece to bottom of cardboard heart.

4. Glue silver braid around seam, starting at top center.

5. Cut 3 pieces of purple fabric 1½" x 3". Fold pieces in half bringing short sides together. Sew a gathering stitch along raw edges and pull to gather. Glue each piece in position as indicated on Diagram 2 on page 67.

6. Cut aqua fabric into 8 assorted circles ⅝" to 1½" in diameter. Hand-gather around edge of circles and place a small ball of stuffing in center. Pull gathering thread and knot but don't cut thread. Push needle up through middle and knot off. Sew or glue into position on heart.

7. To form bead strands, use 20 to 35 beads per strand. Draw thread through all beads. Count up 6 beads from bottom and reinsert needle back up through all beads. Tie off. Continue for 8 strands. Glue into place according to Diagram 2 on page 67.

8. Make 5 rosettes; see "Ribbon/ Fabric Rosette" on page 15. Sew beads in center of rosettes and glue in place on heart.

Pattern for Violets and Lavender

Diagram 1

Diagram 2

Ribbon Sachet

Beads On Blue

MATERIALS

Two 3" squares of blue velvet fabric; matching thread
1000 lt.-colored seed beads
200 dk.-colored seed beads
Stuffing
Beading needles

DIRECTIONS

1. To form pincushion, match wrong sides of velvet squares and sew ¼" seams, leaving a 2" opening for stuffing. Stuff firmly and slipstitch closed.

2. Transfer leaf pattern from Diagram 1 on page 71 onto pincushion, using basting stitches or an air-soluble marker.

3. Begin beading by threading 4 lt.-colored beads onto a double-threaded beading needle which has been brought up through the center of the design. Form a loop by inserting needle back into center. Repeat same step with 4 more beads. This will provide a raised center for the design.

4. Beginning at the center of one leaf figure, draw the thread through. Thread 8 beads on needle and insert needle on the left edge of leaf; see Diagram 1. Bring needle out at the center of the leaf and begin threading beads again. (Work in rows indicated by center lines on the pattern. As the rows get smaller, fewer beads are needed to fill the area. The beads are not precisely the same on each side, so use only the number of beads you need to fill the area. Work from left base to point and from point to right base before moving on to the next petal. Bring the needle up in the center after inserting in at the edge every time. Always bead from the center out.)

5. For corners, bring needle up and thread with 14 dk.-colored beads. Take needle through first 3 beads threaded and pull tight to form a circle. Secure circle to pincushion by taking 2 or 3 small stitches over the beading thread. Form circle with 20 light beads the same way, securing circle around the center circle. Continue on each of the 4 corners.

6. For center of leaves, bring thread up in center of design. Thread 16 beads on needle and insert needle about ½" from point of leaf, exactly where the beads that form the point of the leaf begin. This will form a raised loop-like stamen. Bring needle up through center again and repeat for all leaves.

7. Bring needle out to the left of seam about ¾" from corner. Thread 3 beads and whipstitch to edge, bringing needle out to the left again. Repeat approximately 11 times along the edge of cushion. Repeat beaded whipstitching around the remaining edges of cushion.

Pin-stuck

MATERIALS

Two 5" squares of white satin fabric
600 gilt ½" straight pins
500 white seed beads
500 gold seed beads
100 white sequins
Stuffing
Tacky glue

DIRECTIONS

1. Sew satin squares, right sides together, leaving ½" opening for stuffing. Stuff firmly and slipstitch opening closed.

2. Baste both diagonals from corner to corner to find center of pincushion.

3. Using pin-stuck pattern on page 71, mark a ⅝" square in the very center of basting lines. These lines will be the guides for the pinwork. The center square is at a diagonal to the pincushion itself.

4. Begin at one corner and thread a gold bead on pin. Dip pin into glue and place pin in cushion. Seven pins will equal ⅝" when placed side by side. Use diagram for placement of pins, always checking that the pins form straight lines and the diagonals guide the work from the center outward.

5. Finish the corners with sequins and light beads, beginning in the corner and working toward the center. Filling each corner requires about 15 pins.

Ribbon Sachet

MATERIALS

10" square of white satin fabric; matching thread
6½" square of white satin fabric
10" square stabilizer
3 yards of lightweight ½" white silk ribbon with gold threads
30" of pearl piping
30" of white velvet piping
Assorted pearls for embellishment
Stuffing
Air-soluble marker
Glue gun and glue sticks
Machine embroidery foot
6" to 8" embroidery hoop

DIRECTIONS

1. Transfer ribbon pattern on page 71 to center of 10" satin square, using air-soluble marker.

2. Layer the fabric and stabilizer, design up, over the larger embroidery hoop. Place the smaller hoop inside (this is backward from regular embroidery) so that the design will lay flat against the surface of the sewing machine.

3. With one end of the ribbon, take a few small stitches at point 1 to secure. With presser foot down, feed dogs up, and using small stitches, stitch down the middle of the ribbon following the design. Use the hoop to manipulate fabric under the presser foot. The ribbon may be flipped at points to form leaves. Be careful not to catch layers of previously sewn ribbon. Design is one continuous line. End design at point 2.

4. Trim 10" square down to 6½", centering design.

5. Baste pearl piping using narrow zipper foot ¼" away from raw edge. Baste velvet piping in the same manner but resting the piping above the pearls.

6. Baste back of cushion to front with right sides together and leaving an opening for turning. Clip corners. Turn and stuff firmly. Slipstitch opening closed.

7. Glue assorted pearls to front of cushion.

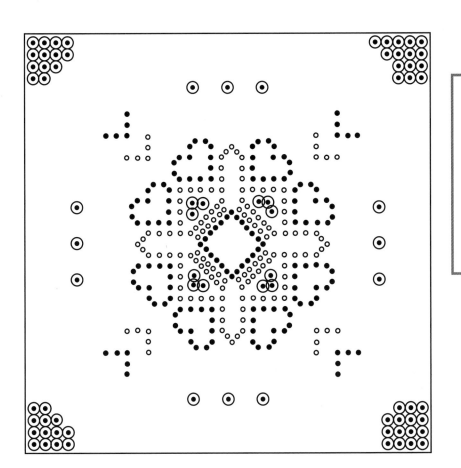

Pattern for Pin-stuck

KEY TO PIN-STUCK

○ = Gold Pin,
       White Bead

● = Gold Pin,
       Gold Bead

⊙ = Gold Pin,
       White Bead,
       Sequin

Pattern for Ribbon Sachet

Pattern for Beads On Blue

Diagram 1

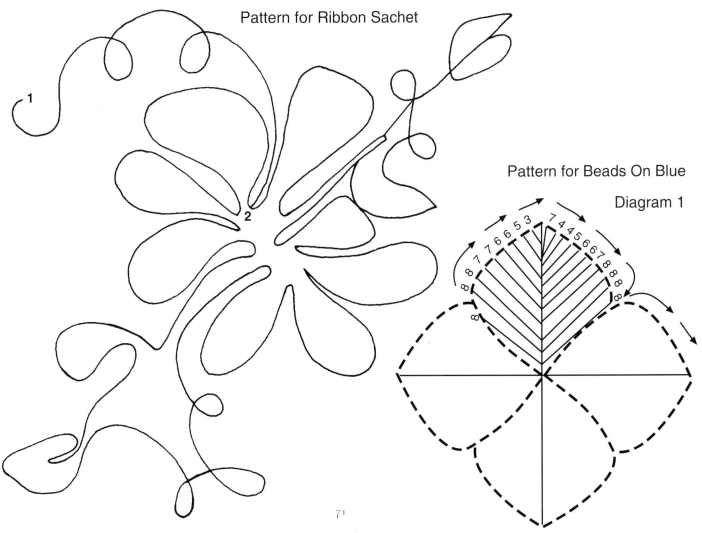

Terra Cotta Saucers

MATERIALS
9" circle of tapestry fabric
Clay pot saucer
Deco Art Clear-tex (texturizing medium)
Acrylic paint to match fabric
Embellishments: bead strands, doily
    pieces, lace, braid, buttons, charms
Stuffing
Glue gun and glue sticks

DIRECTIONS
1. Following manufacturer's instructions on texturizing medium, mix with acrylic paint of desired color. Paint clay saucer and let dry.

2. Sew a ¼" gathering stitch around the outside of fabric circle. Pull to gather

slightly. Stuff firmly and close opening. Hot-glue cushion into clay saucer.

3. Embellish as in photo or as desired.

Lapel Pin

MATERIALS

3" metal bolo tie cone
18" of flat scalloped 2" lace
5" circle of satin
4mm silk ribbon:
    1½ yards of dk. green
    12" of 4 different colors of rose
Cherub charm
5" lapel pin
Stuffing

DIRECTIONS

1. Sew a gathering stitch ¼" on straight side of lace. Pull tightly. Glue to inside of cone.

2. Sew a ¼" gathering stitch around 5" satin circle. Gather loosely and stuff firmly. Pull threads tight and tie off. Place in center of lace. Sew to lace from back side.

3. Make a 5-looped bow with dk. green ribbon and glue to bottom front. Cascade two of the tails around edges of satin; see "Cascading" on page 14.

4. Make 10 ribbon rosettes; see "Ribbon/Fabric Rosette" on page 15. Secure rosettes around cascading; see photo.

5. Glue lapel pin in bottom of cone.

"There were five peas
they were gre
and so they thou
the whole world m
(Hans Christi

Stick Up Your Heels

MATERIALS

1 high heel shoe
6 assorted sized scraps of interesting lace or fabric
10" x 7" piece of velvet
Felt for bottom of shoe
1 yard of 1½" metallic wired ribbon
1 yard each of 3 different colors of 7mm silk ribbon
9" of 9mm silk ribbon
12" of 1" delicate lace
½ yard of ¾" gathered lace
Brass pieces: double-sided cherub, large fan, fancy filigree shape, filigree heart, large bow, small corner
Stuffing
Glue

DIRECTIONS

1. Cover shoe randomly with lace and fabric scraps. Glue to inside of shoe and to sole of shoe.

2. Wrap heel with some of the metallic ribbon. The ribbon will not wrap cleanly, so just keep tucking the ribbon under as you wrap.

3. Cut velvet oval that is 2" larger all around than the shoe's opening. Sew a ¼" gathering stitch around the outer edge of oval. Pull stitches so that the oval cups. Stuff oval firmly. Stitch to secure.

4. Stuff inside of shoe until you can slip the velvet oval into place without it sinking into the shoe. Glue oval pincushion to shoe at the inside, top edge of shoe.

5. Glue gathered lace around shoe opening below velvet. Do not place any lace at front edge of shoe.

6. Glue fancy filigree to front of shoe. Glue fan to left side of fancy filigree. Make a 4" looped bow with the delicate lace. Glue to right side of fancy filigree.

7. Cut 2 pieces of the metallic ribbon 6½" long. Fold raw edges of ribbon in so that they overlap about ¼" in center. Pinch center together and glue. Repeat with other ribbon. Place bows diagonally across each other, forming an X and glue together.

8. Using the remaining metallic ribbon, fold ribbon in half so that it measures ¾" instead of 1½". Sew a gathering stitch along the folded edge of ribbon. Pull threads to gather, making a half-circle ruffle. Glue ribbon ruffle to base of fancy filigree.

9. Lay the 3 lengths of 7mm silk ribbon together and make a bow. Glue to center of metallic bow. Tie knots in tails about every 2". Cascade the tails down toward front of shoe, gluing the knots along the lace/velvet line; see Ribbon Work on page 14.

10. With 9mm silk ribbon, make a rosette; see "Ribbon/Fabric Rosette" on page 15. Glue to center of bow.

11. Glue large filigree heart and bow to front of shoe below metallic ribbon ruffle. Glue small corner to toe of shoe. Let dry.

Rose Wristband

MATERIALS

Leaves
Two 3" x 6½" strips of green velvet
3" x 6½" strip of fleece

Wristband
Two 2" x 17" strips of green velvet
2" x 17" strip of fleece
7" piece of ½" elastic

Rosette
Two 2" x 19" strips of purple velvet
2" x 19" strip of fleece

DIRECTIONS

1. Cut two leaves from green velvet, using Pattern C (Pineapple leaf) on page 91. Stitch ¼" seam, leaving opening to turn. Turn and whipstitch opening closed. Do not press. Sew a running stitch from one point of leaf to the other end, gathering slightly.

2. For wristband, place right sides of green velvet strips together. Put fleece strip on top. Stitch two parallel lines on long sides. Turn. Stitch two topstitching parallel lines ½" from each side to make elastic casing. Pull elastic through center seams. Sew two ends of elastic together. Whipstitch ends of velvet band together.

3. For rosette, place the purple velvet right sides together. Place fleece on top. Stitch around, leaving a 2" opening to turn. Trim off excess fleece. Turn and stitch closed. Make fabric rosette; see "Ribbon/Fabric Rosette" on page 15.

4. Tack leaves to bottom of rosette. Tack rosette and leaves to wristband.

Ribbon Bonnet

See photo on page 78.

MATERIALS
5" doll's straw hat
3" square piece of cardboard
17" x 5" ivory fabric strip
Two 6" circles of velvet
½ yard of cream gathered lace
24" of 1" cream lace
1 yard of ⅝" sheer ribbon
½ yard of 1" wired ribbon
½ yard of narrow braid
Stamen
Silver charms: cherub, filigree heart,
    bow with small heart
Stuffing
Tacky glue or glue gun and
    glue sticks

DIRECTIONS
1. Cut crown off of straw hat, leaving ½" above brim.

2. Measure the outer edge of the hat's brim to determine the exact measurement of fabric you will need. Beginning at the inside, center back of hat, glue one long edge of fabric to the inside base of the crown. The fabric will fit the outer brim of the hat, so you will need to finger-pleat the strip around the crown base as you glue. Extend the fabric strip to the top side of the hat. Glue the top edge of fabric to the base of the crown, finger-pleating as you glue.

3. Cut an oval from the cardboard so that it fits on the underside of the hat brim.

Cover oval with velvet. Glue to underside.

4. Sew a ¼" gathering stitch around outer edge of the other velvet circle. Pull to gather and stuff so that it will fit onto crown of hat. Sliptitch to secure.

5. Place a small amount of stuffing inside hat; then place the velvet ball so that it sits above the base of the crown. Glue.

6. Glue or sew gathered lace to inside edge of hat brim.

7. Glue lace around base of crown, gathering as you go. Glue braid around center of lace.

Hats Abound

See photo on page 79.

MATERIALS
5½" circle of cardboard
½ yard of satin, taffeta, or crepe fabric
2" square of tulle or very fine lace fabric
1 yard of 2" lace
½ yard of ¼" braid for outer edge of
    brim
Embellishments: 1 yard of 2" sheer
    ribbon, 1 yard of 1" sheer ribbon,
    silk flowers, velvet berries, wired
    leaves, ½ yard of 7mm silk ribbon,
    11 yards of 4mm silk ribbon, buttons
Stuffing
Glue gun and glue sticks

DIRECTIONS
1. For hat brim, cut one 11" circle from fabric. Hand-sew a gathering stitch ¼" from edge. Pull gradually. Before gathering tightly, slip cardboard circle inside. Gather fabric around cardboard and center before securing ends of thread. Brim can be used either with gathers on top or bottom. Secure center with a dab of hot glue. Add an appliqué, button, or piece of braid, if using gathers on bottom of brim.

2. For hat crown, cut one 6½" circle from fabric. Gather by hand ¼" from edge. Stuff as firmly as desired. Both loose and firm packs are attractive.

3. Glue crown, gathered side down, at very center of brim.

4. Cut one 11" circle from tulle or lace. Center circle over crown and tie a fine piece of thread around spot where crown meets the brim. Space the gathers evenly around brim. Make certain tulle doesn't hug crown snugly. There should be space between tulle and fabric.

Ivory Hat
Follow Steps 1 through 4. Trim lace ⅜" larger than brim. Bring a thread up from bottom through center of crown, attach a button, and tightly pull thread back down through crown to bottom. Begin gluing braid to outer edge of brim, catching edge of lace. This will make the lace "pouf" a little on the brim. Continue gluing around brim in same manner, easing in fullness of lace. Begin at center point of five 2-yard lengths of 4mm ribbon together in different colors and loop three

times. Glue base of loops to base of crown. Cascade ribbon tails around one side of hat crown and brim; see Ribbon Work on page 14. Glue silk flowers and leaves randomly around same side of hat.

Rose Hat
Follow Steps 1 through 4. Fold a 32" x 5" piece of lace or tulle in half lengthwise. Hand-sew a gathering stitch along raw edges of strip. Gather to fit around base of crown. Glue where crown and brim meet. Glue velvet berries to crown base. Trim with 1" and 2" sheer ribbon and bows.

Olive Hat
Follow Steps 1 through 4. Sew a gathering stitch lengthwise through center of 18" of 1" sheer ribbon. Gather slightly. Secure to base of crown as hat band by placing 12" of 4mm silk ribbon over gather line and tie around hat. Randomly attach pearl beads to ribbon. Glue velvet leaves and flowers around brim. Trim with bows of 1" sheer ribbon and 9mm silk ribbon, allowing tails to fall freely.

Ribbon Bonnet

Ballet Slippers

MATERIALS

8" x 24" piece of dk. green taffeta;
   matching thread
16" x 8" piece of lt. brown silk fabric;
   matching thread
8" x 12" piece of interfacing
12" of ¾" burgundy wired ribbon
¾ yard of ½" gold ribbon
½ yard of ⅝" stiff gold-edged ribbon
⅜ yard of 2" dk. green sheer organdy
   ribbon
4mm silk ribbon:
   ⅝ yard each of 3 different rose
      colors
   2 yards of gold
   1 yard of dk. green
   1 yard of burgundy
⅝ yard of 7mm dk. green silk ribbon
24 pearls
Stuffing
Tacky glue

DIRECTIONS

Slippers

1. From green taffeta, cut 4 pieces from
slipper pattern and 2 pieces from slipper
sole pattern on page 82. Cut 2 interfacing
pieces from slipper pattern.

2. Place 2 taffeta slipper patterns on top
of each other, right sides together. Place
1 interfacing slipper pattern on top of
this. Sew ¼" around inside seam. Turn
and press. Open heel and stitch, right
sides together. Turn back inside. Sew 2
pleats in toe.

3. Turn slipper inside out and sew sole
around bottom edge. Turn back to right
side and topstitch around opening.
Repeat with second shoe.

Finishing

1. Cut dk. green organdy ribbon in half
and form a bow from each half. (Overlap
ends into center and stitch with gathering
stitch.) Glue bows in place on toes of
slippers.

2. Cut three 4" pieces from burgundy
wired ribbon. Bring short ends together
and sew a ¼" seam on each piece. Pinch
and glue one edge, forming a flower.
Fluff petals so that they curl up.

3. Cut three 9" pieces of gold ribbon.
Form each piece into a circular ruffle and
stitch. Glue to center of burgundy flowers to create bachelor buttons. Glue one
flower onto center of bows on toe of each
slipper.

4. Cut two 9" pieces of gold-edged ribbon. Form each into a circular ruffle and
stitch. Glue one to the left side of bachelor button on the right slipper and the
other to the right side on the left slipper.

5. Cut two 18" pieces of gold silk ribbon.
Tie a tiny bow in each piece, leaving tails
that are about 6" on one side and 10" on
the other side. Glue knot of bow on the
other side of dk. green bows, opposite
gold ruffles. Cascade long tail up the
outer slipper edge; see Ribbon Work on
page 14. Bring short tail up the opposite
side and cascade 3 stitches up inner edge.
On the outer edge, bead cascaded stitches
with 2 pearls.

6. With rose-colored ribbons, make 12
rosettes; see Ribbon/Fabric Rosette on
page 15. Glue 3 rosettes to each tiny gold
bow. Glue one rosette on each cascaded
stitch on inner edge of slipper.

7. Cut one 12½" piece and one 10" piece
of dk. green silk ribbon. Glue one end of
the 12½" piece at the inside sole seam of
each shoe opposite the other ribbon. Tie
ribbons together in the center, leaving a
loop in one of the ribbons for an orna-
ment hanger.

8. Glue remaining bachelor button over
knot in ribbon.

9. Use 1 yard each of gold, burgundy,
and dk. green silk ribbon and holding
strands together, tie a 3" bow. Glue bow
to back of bachelor button. Tie 2 knots at
different intervals on each side, knotting
all 3 tails together. Glue each knot to the
sole seam, spacing so that the ribbons fall
gracefully and frame the slippers.

10. Cut brown silk fabric in half. Fold
each piece in half and sew a seam with
right sides together to form a tube. Sew a
gathering stitch along both raw ends.
Turn. Pull one end closed and secure.
Stuff lightly and secure other end. Repeat
with other piece of fabric. Stuff a "cushion" into each slipper.

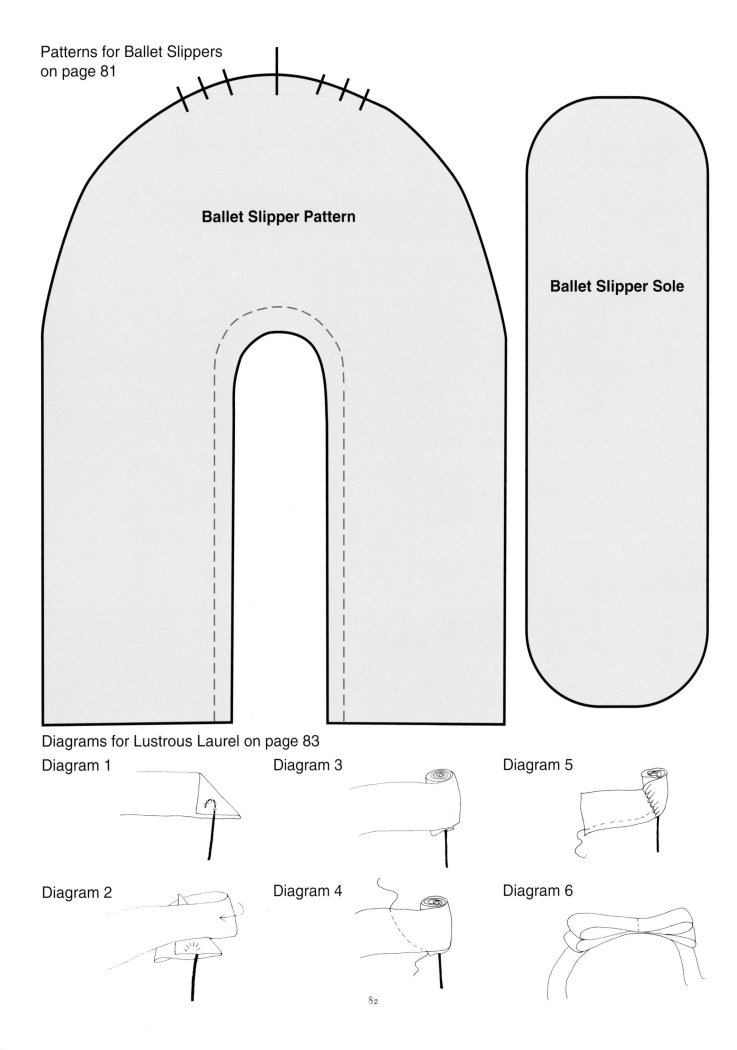

Patterns for Ballet Slippers
on page 81

Ballet Slipper Pattern

Ballet Slipper Sole

Diagrams for Lustrous Laurel on page 83

Diagram 1

Diagram 3

Diagram 5

Diagram 2

Diagram 4

Diagram 6

Lustrous Laurel

See photo on page 84.

MATERIALS
8"-diameter circular wire wreath base
1¼ yards of ¾" green wired ribbon
¾ yard of ¼" red velvet ribbon
¾ yard of 1½" gold metallic wired
   ribbon; matching thread
1⅛ yards of 1½" burgundy wired ribbon;
   matching thread
⅝ yard of 1½" dk. rose wired ribbon;
   matching thread
1½ yards of 1½" green wired ribbon
⅛ yard each of 1½" ribbons:
   burgundy velvet, rose velvet, coral,
   red/yellow pin dot, multi-colored
   print; matching threads
⅝ yard of ¾" dk. green wired ribbon;
   matching thread
1 yard of ⅛" gold cord
⅜ yard of ¼" lt. green ribbon
2½" x ⅛" piece of floral wrapping paper
40" length of 18-gauge wire
Green florist's tape
Stuffing
Glue gun and glue sticks
Needle nose pliers

DIRECTIONS
1. Glue one end of ¾" green wired ribbon to base. Working on a slight slant, wrap ribbon tightly around base, allowing ribbon edges to overlap. Secure with glue on underside of ribbon. Ending at starting point, trim excess and glue opposite end of ribbon in place. Glue one end of red velvet ribbon to wreath at starting point of green ribbon. Working in the opposite direction to green ribbon and on a slight slant, coil velvet ribbon around wreath. Leave about 1" between coils to create striped effect; see photo on page 84. Secure with glue on underside of ribbon. Ending at starting point, trim excess and glue opposite end of ribbon in place. Treat starting and ending points of ribbons as bottom center of wreath.

2. For berries, cut one 4" length from each color of 1½" ribbon except green wired ribbon and dk. rose wired ribbon. From 18-gauge wire, cut eight 5"-long pieces for stems. Wrap stems in florist's

tape. Using needle nose pliers, bend a small hook in one end of each stem.

3. To make one berry, use one 4" length of ribbon and one stem. With right sides facing, sew ends of ribbon together. Sew a gathering stitch along one long edge. Pull thread as tightly as possible; secure. Glue hook end of stem to wrong side of ribbon in center of gathers. Turn ribbon. Stuff firmly, keeping stem in center. Sew a gathering thread along ungathered edge of ribbon. Pull thread as tightly as possible around stem; secure. Repeat with remaining 4" ribbon lengths and stems to make seven berries; reserve one stem.

4. For large rose center, cut one 10" length from gold metallic wired ribbon. Wrap reserved 5" piece of wire with florist's tape. Use needle nose pliers to bend a small hook in one end.

5. To make large rose center, fold one end of gold metallic ribbon over, making a 1½"-wide triangle; see Diagram 1 on page 82. Slide hook end of stem into folded portion; sew in place through both layers of ribbon; see Diagram 1. Roll 4½" of ribbon from right to left, forming a bud; see Diagrams 2 and 3. Sew a gathering stitch along a curve on unrolled ribbon, beginning at top edge about 2½" from rose center and ending at rose center on bottom top edge of remaining ribbon; see Diagram 4. Tighten thread and secure. Sew a gathering stitch along bottom edge of remaining ribbon; see Diagram 5. Pull thread tightly around stem and secure. Fluff petals as desired.

6. For center petals of large rose, cut five 4½" pieces from burgundy wired ribbon. To make petals, sew a gathering stitch along one edge of each length. Tighten thread slightly, shaping lengths into petals; do not secure thread. Fold two petals around rose center, tighten thread, and secure around stem at base of rose center. Fold remaining three petals around first two petals, tighten thread, and secure around stem at base of rose center.

7. For outer petals of large rose, cut one 18" length each from dk. rose wired ribbon and ¾" dk. green wired ribbon. To make petal, sew a gathering stitch along one long edge of dk. rose ribbon. Tighten thread; do not secure. Arrange petal around stem, pushing snugly up against center petals and secure. Repeat with dk. green ribbon.

8. For small rose, cut one 10" length from dk. rose ribbon and two 4½" lengths from gold metallic wired ribbon. To make rose center, repeat Step 5, using dk. rose wired ribbon and omitting stem. To make petals, repeat Step 7, using gold metallic wired ribbon. Glue rose center in middle of petals.

9. To make green bow, fold 1½" green wired ribbon into four 6"-long loops, leaving 12"-long tails on each side. Sew through center to secure loops; see Diagram 6. Set aside.

10. To make paper fan, fold wrapping paper piece so that short edges match. Make ¼"-wide accordion folds in one-half of wrapping paper. Turn paper; repeat with other half. Pinch bottom edges of folds together and open out fan; glue bottom edges in place.

11. Wrap stems of five berries around wreath, clustering them left of center at bottom. Wrap stems of large rose and remaining berries around wreath, positioning them right of center at bottom. Glue to secure. Glue center of green bow to bottom center of wreath. Loosely coil bow tails around wreath, gluing as necessary. Notch ends. Beginning and ending underneath bow, loosely coil and fold cord around wreath and bow tails, gluing to secure. Wrap ¼" lt. green ribbon tightly around center of bow and around wreath to left and right of bow, covering ends of stems. Glue small rose to center of bow. Glue fan to bow below small rose.

Maize

See photo on page 85.

MATERIALS

12"-square piece of white satin
Two 12"-square pieces of fleece
4 yards of 3" white ribbon
Sewing thread: green and gold
Acrylic paint: gold, lt. brown, yellow,
    3 shades of green
Corn silk or similar fiber
Liquid starch
3 eye droppers
Toothpicks
Newspapers
Plastic garbage bag
Spray adhesive
Small squeegee
Large shallow pan

DIRECTIONS

1. Prepare for marbleizing the material by laying out newspapers under a large shallow pan. Place a plastic garbage bag beside pan for fabric to dry on. Pour 2" of liquid starch into pan. Tear some newspapers into strips to use for skimming top of starch. Pour 2 tablespoons each of gold, lt. brown, and yellow paint, separately into 3 plastic cups. Thin paints with enough water to make each the consistency of milk. Skim surface with newspaper.

2. For each color, fill an eyedropper with paint. Carefully float several drops onto starch. (If the paint globs together or sinks, it is too thick. If it disperses too quickly, it is too thin. If either problem occurs, skim paint from surface and try again.) Apply paint until surface is covered with all three colors. With a toothpick, stir or rake the surface only, creating a pattern until you have a desired design.

3. Transfer pattern to fabric by holding both ends of white satin and gently lowering it onto the starch surface, center first and outside edges last. After about 5 seconds, lift corners of fabric and rake along side of pan to remove excess liquid. Place fabric on plastic garbage bag with design side up. Gently squeegee liquid off fabric. Allow to dry. Iron between press cloths to set colors. Repeat process with the white ribbon and green paints.

4. Place the gold-dyed fabric on top of the 2 layers of fleece and sew straight lines down in one direction 1" apart. Hand-stitch across from one line to the next, pulling the thread tightly as you go. Continue stitching by rows, making a corn pattern.

5. With right sides facing, fold over gold material and sew together making a tube. Turn. At the top, sew a gathering stitch and pull tightly. Secure. Repeat with the other end.

6. Apply spray adhesive to corn silk. Roll top half of corn in corn silk leaving 2" to 3" of silk above top of corn. Set aside.

7. With green ribbon, cut one 28" piece and one 34" piece. With right sides together, bring ends in to the middle. Sew a leaf pattern (see diagram). Leaving ¼", cut off excess ribbon. Turn and press. Repeat with other ribbon.

8. Leaving 1½" at the bottom, place leaves up around corn, shorter in front and longer in back. Secure around bottom and tack leaves into place, securing corn silk between corn and leaves.

Diagram

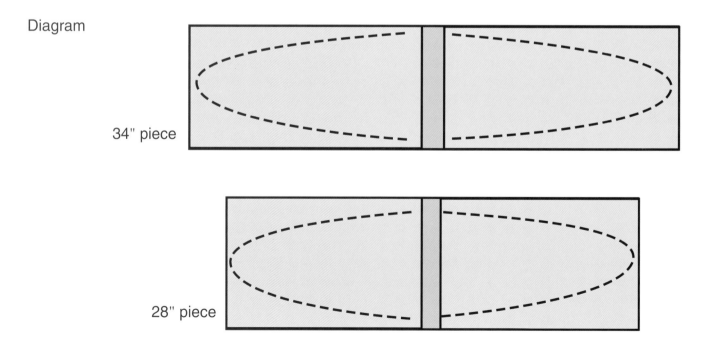

34" piece

28" piece

Fruits Sewn of Love

Pineapple

MATERIALS
14" x 12" piece of yellow velvet
25" x 6" strip of green velvet
25" x 6" strip of fleece
Stuffing

DIRECTIONS
1. From green velvet, cut four pieces using pattern A on page 91, two pieces using pattern B on page 91, and two pieces using pattern C on page 91.

2. To make one leaf, place two pieces from pattern A with right sides together and a piece of fleece on top. Sew ¼" around edges, leaving bottom open to turn. Trim excess fleece and turn. Topstitch ¼" inside of edge. Topstitch again ¼" inside the first row of topstitching. Repeat all for second leaf. Also repeat for leaf from pattern B.

3. Place two pieces from pattern C with right sides together and a piece of fleece on top. Stitch ¼" around edges, leaving opening to turn. Trim excess fleece, turn and stitch closed.

4. Fold leaf C in half lengthwise. Position open end of each remaining leaf sandwiched in the center of this fold with longer leaf (B) at the rear. Pull points of leaf C up toward other leaf points, slightly overlapping sides and forming a point at the bottom. Machine-stitch across this point, securing all ends within leaf C. Set aside.

5. Cut thirty 2" squares from yellow velvet.

6. Finger-press into halves and then in half again. Mark the second fold (center of square) with a pin and unfold second fold; see Diagram P on page 91.

7. Stitch in a continuous line from center of folds on the diagonal to the corner; see Diagram 1.

8. Sew five triangles together with middle seams pointing toward the middle to form the base of the pineapple; see

Diagram 2 on page 91.

9. Sew two sets of ten triangles together, alternating points.

10. Sew the two sets of ten triangles together, matching points. Attach to base, matching seams. Sew remaining triangles as sewn for the base piece, but sew triangles together halfway up. Attach to row of ten, matching seams.

11. Stuff pineapple firmly, filling points.

12. Stitch top of pineapple closed and blind-stitch leaves onto pineapple top.

Velvet Strawberry

MATERIALS (for one strawberry)
4" square of red velvet; matching thread
2" square of leaf-green velvet; matching thread
4 velvet leaves
Gold fabric paint
Florist wire
Stuffing
Glue gun and glue sticks
Thin paint brush

DIRECTIONS
1. Using Velvet Strawberry pattern on page 92, cut one from red velvet. Fold in half, right sides together, and stitch along seam lines into a cone. Turn right side out and stuff. Gather top opening and close with small stitches.

2. Using strawberry top pattern on page 92, cut one from green velvet. Insert velvet leaves through center of strawberry top. Glue velvet leaves to top of strawberry.

3. Curl a piece of florist wire around leaf stems to form tendrils.

4. Dot strawberry with gold paint for seeds.

Painted Strawberry

MATERIALS
4" square piece of red satin fabric; matching thread
3" piece of 2" green velvet ribbon
6" of 1" cream lace
¼" ribbon:
    24" of olive green
    9" of rose
3" of 1" burgundy silk ribbon
Fabric paint: burgundy and gold
1" green covered florist wire
Stuffing
Hot glue gun and glue sticks
Sponge
Thin paintbrush

DIRECTIONS
1. Cut two red satin pieces from Painted Strawberry pattern on page 92. Sponge-paint fabric lightly with burgundy paint. Let dry. Sew, right sides together, leaving top open. Turn inside out and stuff tightly. Sew a gathering stitch around the top and pull tight. Stitch closed.

2. Paint seeds randomly around strawberry with gold paint.

3. From the green velvet ribbon, cut one leaf, using leaf pattern. Glue to top of strawberry.

4. Place florist wire down through top and glue into place for stem.

5. Gather the lace into a semi-circle and sew to top of strawberry.

6. Place two 12" lengths of olive green silk ribbon together and tie a bow in middle. Knot ends. Glue onto bottom of stem.

7. With rose silk ribbon, make one ¼" rosette; see "Ribbon/Fabric Rosette" on page 15. Glue in middle of bow.

8. With burgundy silk ribbon, make a fabric rose; see "Fabric Rose" on page 14. Glue on top of lace.

Fruits Sewn of Love

Velvet Grapes

MATERIALS
14" x 18" piece of white velvet
Purple fabric dye
Purple sewing thread
10" of 1" sheer peach ribbon
Acrylic paint: green, dk. purple, amber,
      lt. brown, and gold
8" piece of grapevine
18" of stem wire
6 small wired leaves
Stuffing
Tacky glue
Plastic bowl for dye
Wire cutters
Paintbrush

DIRECTIONS
All seams ¼".

Dyeing

In a small plastic bowl, prepare dye
according to package instructions. Dye
velvet fabric for 30 seconds, or until
desired color. When rinsing dye, twist
and wring fabric under the tap for an
uneven, textured effect. Let air dry.

1. Dye velvet purple; let dry. Cut fifteen
3" circles from material. Sew a basting
stitch around perimeter of each circle.
Pull thread until fabric forms a cup. Stuff
firmly; pull thread tight and secure.
Repeat with all circles.

2. Paint grapevine green and let dry.
Starting at the top with the largest grapes,
glue gathered side onto grapevine.
Repeat with remaining grapes, putting
the smallest on bottom.

4. Cut three 6" pieces of stem wire.
Attach each to grapevine as desired and
wrap ends around a pencil to curl for tendrils. Glue 3 wired leaves together to
make grape leaves. Repeat with 3
remaining leaves. Glue "grape leaves" to
grapevine where grapes start.

5. Highlight grapes with dk. purple and
amber. Highlight leaves with lt. brown,
green and gold. Highlight stem and tendrils with gold. Tie sheer ribbon around
stem.

Velvet Pear

MATERIALS
7" x 15" piece of white velvet
Fabric dye: lt. green
Sewing thread: green
10" of 1" sheer peach ribbon
Acrylic paint bright yellow, yellow,
      yellow-green, lt. brown, green, and
      gold
8" of stem wire
1 small wired leaf
Stuffing
Plastic bowl for dye
Wire cutters
Paintbrush

DIRECTIONS
All seams ¼".

Dyeing

In a small plastic bowl, prepare dye
according to package instructions. Dye
velvet fabric for 30 seconds, or until
desired color. When rinsing dye, twist
and wring fabric under the tap for an
uneven, textured effect. Let air dry.

1. Dye velvet lt. green and let dry. Cut
two Pear pattern pieces found on page 92
from velvet. Pin pear sections, right sides
together, at edges. Stitch sections together, leaving an opening for stuffing. Turn
and stuff firmly.

2. Paint an 8" piece of stem wire gold.
When dry, insert through top center of
pear and out the bottom. Push end back
up through center, leaving about ½" of
loop at bottom. Bend wire over at bottom
to secure.

3. Highlight pear with bright yellow, yellow, and yellow-green. Highlight one
leaf with lt. brown and green. Let dry.
Glue leaf to stem. Tie sheer ribbon
around stem.

Velvet Peach

MATERIALS
7" x 14" piece of white velvet
Tan and lt. green fabric dye
Orange sewing thread
6" of 1" sheer peach ribbon
6" of stem wire
Acrylic paint: orange, lt. brown, and
      green
2 small wired leaves
Stuffing
Plastic bowl for dye
Wire cutters
Paintbrush

DIRECTIONS
All seams ¼".

Dyeing

In a small plastic bowl, prepare dye
according to package instructions. Dye
velvet fabric for 30 seconds, or until
desired color. When rinsing dye, twist
and wring fabric under the tap for an
uneven, textured effect. Let air dry.

1. Dye velvet lt. green then tan; let dry.
Using pattern on page 92, cut 6 peach
pieces from orange velvet. Sew 3 sections together. Repeat with other 3 sections. Sew the 2 halves, right sides
together, leaving an opening for stuffing.
Turn and stuff firmly.

2. Paint and insert 6" of stem wire gold.
When dry, insert through top center of
peach and out the bottom. Push end back
up through center, leaving about ½" of
loop at bottom. Bend wire over at bottom
to secure.

3. Highlight peach with orange paint.
Highlight two leaves with lt. brown and
green. Let dry. Glue leaves to stem. Tie
sheer ribbon around stem.

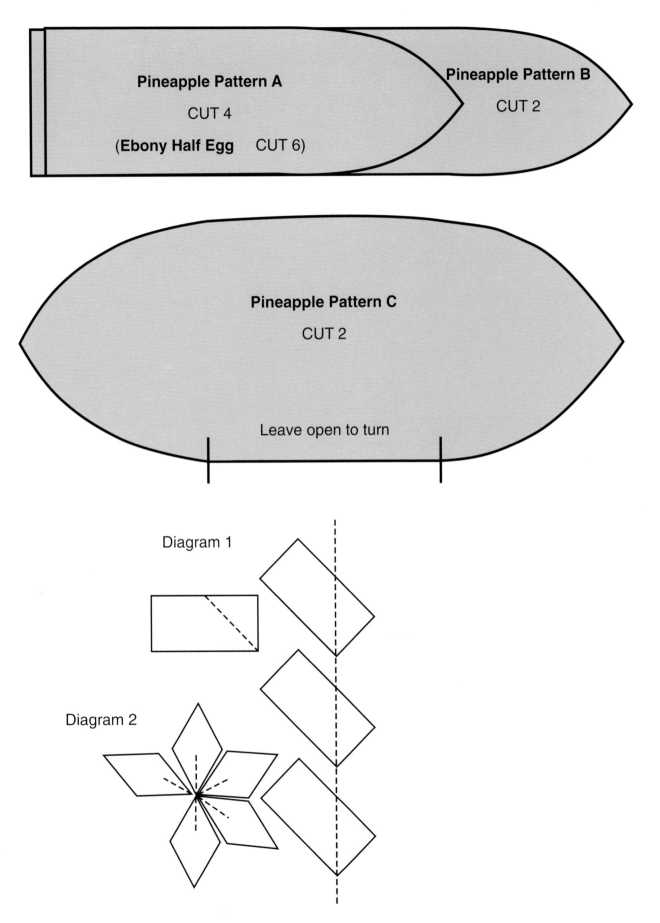

Pineapple Pattern A

CUT 4

(**Ebony Half Egg** CUT 6)

Pineapple Pattern B

CUT 2

Pineapple Pattern C

CUT 2

Leave open to turn

Diagram 1

Diagram 2

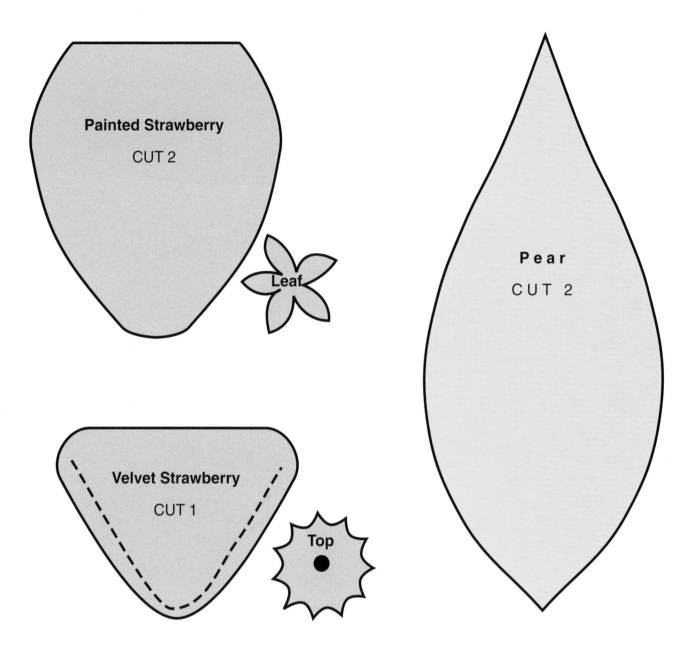

Painted Strawberry

CUT 2

Leaf

P e a r

C U T 2

Velvet Strawberry

CUT 1

Top

Pattern for Velvet Peach on page 90

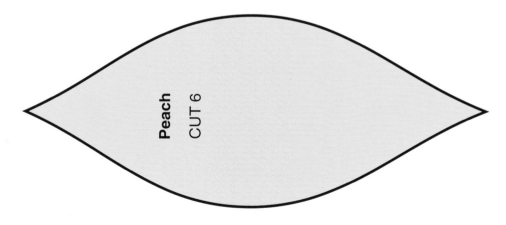

Peach CUT 6

Dollhouse Faire

MATERIALS (for one chair)
Finished design
Purchased dollhouse chair
Lightweight cardboard
Stuffing
Glue gun and glue sticks

DIRECTIONS
1. Remove original cushion from purchased dollhouse chair. Measure cushion and select a suitable finished design size from the cross-stitch patterns below to fit area of cushion.

2. Using cushion as a pattern, center finished design and cut around, adding ½" for seam. From pattern, cut one piece of lightweight cardboard.

3. Sew a ¼" gathering stitch along edge of finished design. Pull threads slightly. Place a ball of stuffing in center of wrong side of fabric. Stuff firmly.

4. Insert cardboard piece. Pull threads tightly and tie off.

5. Glue cross-stitch cushion to chair seat.

Grape Leaves

Stitched on cream Belfast linen 32 over 2 threads. The finished design size is 1¼" x 1¼". The fabric was cut 6" x 6".

FABRIC	DESIGN SIZES
Aida 11	1⅞" x 1⅞"
Aida 14	1⅜" x 1⅜"
Aida 18	1⅛" x 1⅛"
Hardanger 22	⅞" x ⅞"

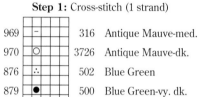

Anchor		DMC (used for sample)	
Step 1: Cross-stitch (1 strand)			
969	-	316	Antique Mauve-med.
970	O	3726	Antique Mauve-dk.
876	∴	502	Blue Green
879	●	500	Blue Green-vy. dk.

Anchor		DMC (used for sample)	
Step 2: Backstitch (1 strand)			
879		500	Blue Green-vy. dk.

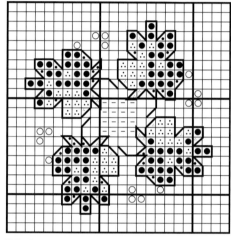

Stitch count: 20 x 20

Wreath

Stitched on platinum Belfast linen 32 over 1 thread. The finished design size is 1⅝" x 1⅝". The fabric was cut 6" x 6".

FABRIC	DESIGN SIZES
Aida 11	2⅜" x 2⅜"
Aida 14	1⅞" x 1⅞"
Aida 18	1½" x 1½"
Hardanger 22	1⅛" x 1⅛"

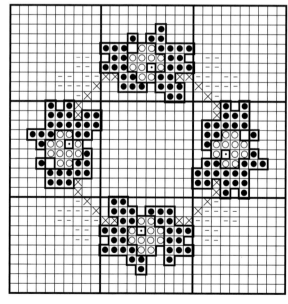

Stitch count: 26 x 26

Anchor		DMC (used for sample)	
Step 1: Cross-stitch (1 strand)			
301	·	744	Yellow-pale
894	O	223	Shell Pink-med.
858	-	524	Fern Green-vy. lt.
859	●	522	Fern Green
882	X	407	Pecan

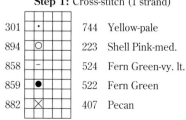
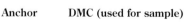

Anchor		DMC (used for sample)	
Step 2: Backstitch (1 strand)			
897		221	Shell Pink-vy. dk.
246		319	Pistachio Green-vy. dk.

94

Daisy

Stitched on white Belfast linen 32 over 1 thread. The finished design size is 1¾" x 2". The fabric was cut 6" x 6".

FABRIC	DESIGN SIZES
Aida 11	2½" x 2⅞"
Aida 14	2" x 2¼"
Aida 18	1½" x 1¾"
Hardanger 22	1¼" x 1⅜"

Anchor   **DMC (used for sample)**

Step 1: Cross-stitch (1 strand)

Anchor		DMC	
386	·	746	Off White
301	–	744	Yellow-pale
297	O	743	Yellow-med.
215	△	320	Pistachio Green-med.
246	▲	319	Pistachio Green-vy. dk.
347	X	402	Mahogany-vy. lt.
338	∴	3776	Mahogany-lt.

Step 2: Backstitch (1 strand)

246		319	Pistachio Green-vy. dk.
338		3776	Mahogany-lt.

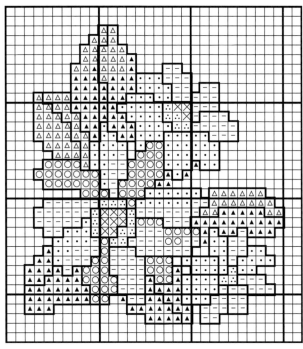

Stitch count: 28 x 31

Salmon Roses

Stitched on white Belfast linen 32 over 1 thread. The finished design size is 1⅞" x 2⅛". The fabric was cut 6" x 6".

FABRIC	DESIGN SIZES
Aida 11	2¾" x 3⅛"
Aida 14	2⅛" x 2⅜"
Aida 18	1⅝" x 1⅞"
Hardanger 22	1⅜" x 1½"

Anchor   **DMC (used for sample)**

Step 1: Cross-stitch (1 strand)

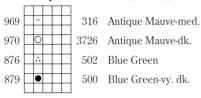

969	–	316	Antique Mauve-med.
970	O	3726	Antique Mauve-dk.
876	∴	502	Blue Green
879	●	500	Blue Green-vy. dk.

Step 2: Backstitch (1 strand)

879		500	Blue Green-vy. dk.

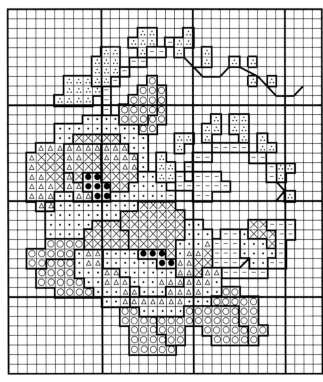

Stitch count: 30 x 34

Tin Wicker

MATERIALS

4½" x 3" empty tin can (without ripples)
    for chair
3½" x 2" empty tin can (without ripples)
    for footstool
6" circle of print fabric
4" circle of print fabric
3" circle of heavy cardboard
2" circle of heavy cardboard
Fine permanent marking pen
White glossy spray paint
Stuffing
Glue gun and glue sticks
Tin snips
Extra-slim needle nose pliers

DIRECTIONS

1. Cut off bottom of each tin can with tin snips. With fine marking pen, score vertical lines at ⅛" intervals around each can. Cut along lines with tin snips.

2. For chair, count off 16 consecutive strips. Snip off the seventh, eighth, ninth and tenth strips. Set aside. The 12 strips remaining will serve as the front legs of the chair.

3. Using needle nose pliers, bend left three consecutive strips on each leg outward toward the left (almost perpendicular to the can top). Bend the right three strips outward toward the right. For each leg, position the six strips on top of each other. Secure together by wrapping snipped off strip piece around six strips about ¾" down from top of can, pinch, and snip close.

4. With needle nose pliers, begin rolling (as you do with hair curlers) the first strip of each leg up to the secured point. Repeat for the sixth strip in opposite direction. Return to second strip and roll

until touching the bottom of first roll. Return to fifth and roll until touching the bottom of the sixth roll. Return to third and roll up until touching the bottom of the second roll. Return and repeat for the fourth strip until touching the bottom of the fifth roll.

5. Directly opposite the open space between the front legs, center and count off five strips. Bend these strips upward over the can top with the first two strips toward the left and the remaining three strips bending toward the right. Butt together and secure as in Step 3. This area will serve as the chair back.

6. Position third strip of chair back straight up. Snip at about 2½" from top of can. Loop second and fourth strips up, curling toward and hiding the top of the third (creating a heart shape). Secure these together as above, allowing for rolling once on each end. Loop first and fifth strips up, curling toward respective sides of heart shape. Secure as above about three quarters of the way up (creating a fan shape). Curl ends.

7. On each side of the chair back, snip off one strip. Count off two, bend these upward over the top of the can, bend toward each other, butt together, and secure as above. Secure again about ½" above the first secured point. Loop inside strips on each side of chair back up and toward the chair back. Secure as above to fan shape about three quarters of the way up. Curl ends. Loop outside strips in opposite direction.

8. On each side of chair back, snip next strip. Count off seven consecutive strips. Bend first strip up and over top of can, bend toward right and secure as above

about 1" from top of can to looped strip from Step 6. Curl end of strip from Step 6. The rest of the first strip will serve as the top of the chair arm. Strips two through seven will serve as the back legs. To complete legs, repeat Steps 3 and 4.

9. Count off strips between the front leg and back leg for each side (there should be about nine remaining on each side). Beginning from each front leg, bend first strip up and over top of can, in an S shape, back toward the chair arm strip end. Match ends and secure as above about ½" from ends. Roll both ends down toward chair arm.

10. Snip off every other remaining strip so that there are only three left on each side. Bend these three up and over top of can toward the chair arm strip. Secure as above just below existing secure point on chair arm/back strip. Roll ends (third strip first) up to secure point.

11. Section footstool into four equal parts. Center and count off six strips for each leg. Snip off the third and fourth strip for each. Bend and secure as above the four remaining strips and roll ends upward as above. Roll remaining strips in alternating directions for desired appearance.

12. Spray-paint the chair and footstool. Set aside and let dry.

13. Sew a gathering stitch ¼" from edge of each fabric circle. For chair, place 3" cardboard circle on 6" fabric circle and gather slightly. Stuff firmly. Gather tightly and tie off. Repeat for footstool, using 2" cardboard circle and 4" fabric circle.

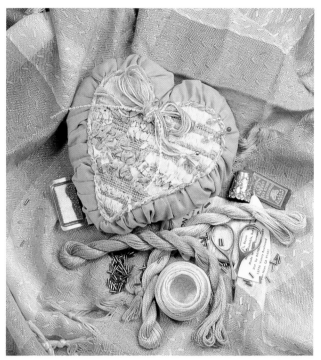

Chapter Two 🐝
Provincial

Pink Pockets

MATERIALS
4" x 8½" strip of print fabric; matching thread
4" x 21" strip of print fabric
4" x 21" strip of contrasting fabric
1 yard of ¼" silk ribbon to match fabrics
22" of 20-gauge wire
A penny
Stuffing
Tacky glue
Glue gun and glue sticks

DIRECTIONS
1. With right sides together, match short ends of 4" x 8½" strip and stitch a ¼" seam, making a tube. Press seam open. Using a fine needle and double thread, make large gathering stitches around top edge about ¼" down. Pull tight and stitch top closed securely. Turn fabric and stuff. Pack tightly. Make gathering stitch again and pull tightly. Before securing, tuck raw edges inside of the cushion. Stitch closed, leaving the length of thread attached to bottom of cushion.

2. With the two remaining strips of contrasting fabric, sew together lengthwise and press seam open. With right sides together, match short ends and stitch a ¼" seam, making a tube. Press seam and turn fabric right side out.

3. Fold in half lengthwise so that the contrasting fabric makes a ¼" border on top of the outside half. Press. Insert length of wire between layers next to the fold line. Machine-stitch ¼" from fold, making a casing for wire.

4. Using a double thread, hand-gather the bottom raw edge ¼" from edge, making sure to catch both layers of fabric. Pull tightly to gather and fasten securely.

5. Using the length of thread at the bottom of cushion, stitch cushion to flower at the inside center.

6. Make 6 even crimps in wired edge and tack to cushion at evenly spaced intervals. Cut silk ribbon into 6 even lengths and make small bows. Glue or stitch bows to cushion at crimped intervals.

7. Cover penny with small circle of fabric and glue to bottom of flower, covering the raw ends of gathers.

Hot Apple Pie

See photo on page 102.

MATERIALS
5" black iron pie rack (ours is heart-shaped)
4" pie tin
6" round piece of apple-print fabric
1½ yards of ⅞" tan muslin ribbon
Fabric fading kit
Antiquing compound for metal
Sandpaper
Brown acrylic paint
Stuffing
Glue gun and glue sticks
Paint brush

DIRECTIONS
1. Follow directions on fabric fading kit to fade the apple-print fabric.

2. Sand parts of pie rack to look old and worn.

3. Brush antiquing compound on pie tin.

4. Run a gathering stitch around edge of apple-print fabric. Pull and gather to make a 4" circle. Stuff lightly. With hot glue gun, glue to inside of pie tin, leaving a 2" opening. Stuff firmly. Glue closed.

5. For the pie crust, hand-tack muslin ribbon around pie tin, making ½" pleats. Glue to make more secure. Lightly brush brown paint along crust.

6. Insert Apple pins found on page 12, in pie.

In the Kitchen

When fall comes, weekend activities tend to move inside. This is when a rustic old kitchen, especially one with a fireplace, can become the focal point for dining. A hearty meal of stuffed cabbage, sweet potatoes, spoonbread, and rich chocolate pie is right at home in such surroundings.

MENU
(for 8)

Pork-and-Apple-Stuffed Cabbage
Steamed Leeks with Red Onion
Fried Sweet Potato Slices
Spoon Bread
Chocolate Custard Pie
Wine
Coffee

The cabbage dish in this menu is inspired by one my grandmother used to cook. Probably it wasn't done this way, but the results are close enough. The filling, I am sure, would adapt itself to many variations of seasoning. When preparing this meal, start with the cabbage, which must steam for 2 hours. The leeks can be steamed in the same pot during the last 45 minutes of cooking time. About halfway through the spoon bread's cooking time, start frying the sweet potatoes. If they finish first, they will hold. Everything should be ready when the spoon bread comes out.

...e custard pie with whipped cream.

The Country Quilter's Companion

Cottage Slipcover

MATERIALS (for one chair)

1¾" x 2" piece of pine for seat
Four 2½" lengths of ¼" dowel for legs
2" x 4" piece of balsa wood for chair
  back
5" x 16" piece of solid fabric for
  slipcover
3" x 12" piece of printed fabric for chair
  cushion
18" x 6" piece of printed fabric for dust
  ruffle
Matching thread
3" x 6" piece of fleece for chair cushion
Braid or ribbon to trim
Glue gun and glue sticks
Drill and ¼" drill bit
Wood glue

DIRECTIONS

1. Cut one chair back from balsa wood, using pattern. Set aside.

2. Drill four holes, according to chair seat pattern, ¼" in underside of chair seat. Insert dowels in holes and secure with wood glue.

3. Glue bottom ¾" of one side of chair back to one long side of chair seat. Set chair aside.

4. Using pattern for Slipcover Back, cut one from solid fabric, adding ¼" for seam allowance. Using pattern, cut one Chair Slipcover Front (with flaps) from solid fabric, adding ¼" all around. Match curved end of these two pieces. With right sides facing, sew ¼" seam around chair back, leaving open at bottom. Clip corners and turn. Slip cover over chair back.

5. Pull flaps tightly and glue to underside

of chair seat, snipping at corners to cover around legs.

6. To make cushion, cut two pieces of printed fabric, according to Chair Cushion pattern, adding ½" for stuffing. Cut one from fleece. Place front and back with right sides together and fleece on wrong side of front piece. Sew ¼" seam around, leaving a 2" opening to turn. Clip corners. Turn and whipstitch closed.

7. Glue back side of chair cushion to slipcover.

8. Fold down 1" from top and up 2" from bottom of fabric piece for dust ruffle. Press and tack edges together. Gather and sew dust ruffle as desired; see photo.

9. Trim as desired.

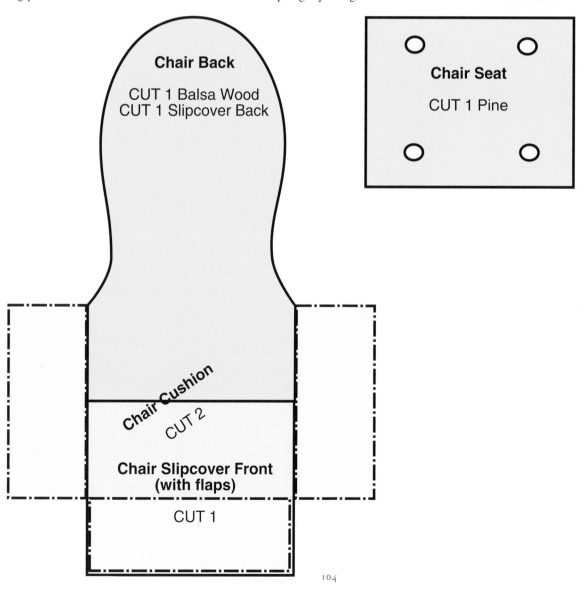

Chair Back

CUT 1 Balsa Wood
CUT 1 Slipcover Back

Chair Seat

CUT 1 Pine

Chair Cushion
CUT 2

**Chair Slipcover Front
(with flaps)**

CUT 1

Keeping Secrets

MATERIALS (for small fabric box)

12" x 30" piece of 1-ply cardboard

Five 5" scraps of old or new embroidery for outside of box

Seven 5" scraps of different fabrics for inside of box and bottom

9" x 22" piece of fabric for remaining box parts

18" x 4" piece of fleece

1 yard of ⅝" ricrac

½ yard of a ⅛" silk ribbon for 2 tiny bows

Charms: scissors, teapot, thimble, 2 old buttons

For the button box:

    12" of matching 2" wired variegated ribbon or 12" each of a 1 ½" ribbon and a ⅝" ribbon

12" of matching narrow trim

4" doily

Tacky glue (add water to thin)

Glue gun and glue sticks

Paintbrush or roller

DIRECTIONS

Preparation

1. Using a photocopy machine, enlarge all patterns on page 109 to 175%. Cut out all cardboard pieces using patterns.

2. Adding ½", cut all fabric pieces using patterns on page 109, and lay the fabric pieces with their corresponding cardboard pieces.

3. Pad with fleece and wrap the following pieces:

    4 inside panels (E)

    1 lid top (D)

    1 inner lid top (F)

    1 inner lid bottom (I)—2 layers of fleece for this piece

Laminating

1. Using thin-bodied glue and a throw-away brush or paint roller, laminate the following pieces with fabric:

    Outer box (A)

    Inside center section of the outer box (A, flipped over)

    Base of box (C)

Inside box bottom (J)
Middle lid (B)
Inner box lid center (H)

2. Laminating fabric onto cardboard is similar to wallpapering. Make sure that fabric is smooth on the cardboard, and that there are no bubbles or air pockets between the layers of fabric and cardboard. Thoroughly covering the cardboard with a coat of glue will eliminate any air bubbles. When wrapping the fabric around the cardboard, make sure to emphasize the shape of the cardboard. Dab extra glue at corners to completely seal the raw edges.

3. Laminating the lid strip: Lay fabric onto work surface, right side down. Paint lid strip with thin layer of glue; then lay lid strip onto fabric, score side down, ¼" above one of the edges, and ½" away from one of the short edges. Smooth fabric completely onto lid strip. Trim away the ¼" worth of fabric flush to the edge of the lid strip. Glue one of the short edges over so that it is flush to the short edge of one side of the lid strip.

4. Laminating the inside box side: Lay fabric onto work surface, right side down. Paint a thin layer of glue onto box side piece; then lay onto fabric, ¼" above one of the long edges, and ½" away from one of the short edges. Smooth fabric completely onto box side. Trim away the ¼" worth of fabric flush to the edge of the box side. Glue one of the short edges over so that it is flush to the short edge of one side of the box side. Trim the other short edge flush to the cardboard.

5. When laminating has dried about 10 minutes, roll the inside box side over a dowel so that the piece of cardboard curves. Also, refold the outside box on the score lines so that the fold is as crisp as possible.

6. Glue the 4 padded sections to the inside of piece A.

Assembly

1. Assemble the lid: Fold flaps of laminated lid down in one direction. Cut a 14" x 2" fabric strip to secure flaps together. Beginning at back center, glue the long edge of the strip around flap

fold. Fold fabric strip under to inside fold and glue all around. Glue small sections at a time. Complete, overlapping short ends, gluing finished end of lid strip on top. Cover inside raw edges with a fabric square cut from pattern D.

2. Glue back center inside flap of lid to the upper edge of the outside box at one of the plus-shaped extensions.

3. Finger-gather trim slightly as you glue it to the top of the edge of the lid. Glue trim to the underside of the box bottom as well.

4. Glue padded lid top over trimmed lid. Glue base to box.

5. Assemble inside box: Glue outer edges of inside box bottom (J) to the inner edge of the box side (G). Complete, overlapping short ends and gluing finished end on top. Flip the extended fabric down over the outside of the box. Glue the excess fabric to the wrong side of the inside box bottom. Trim box side with ribbons. Glue inside box to the inside center of the outside box.

6. Glue wrong side of lid bottom (I) to right side of middle lid (H). Glue inner box lid (F) to middle lid. Stretch and glue doily over lid. Embellish lid with tea pot, yo-yos and bow.

7. Embellish lid of outer box with scissors, thimble, buttons, bow and ricrac flower.

Variations
From this basic pattern for the small box, you can create your own variation on the theme.

We show how we made the same box just a bit larger with a smaller fold-up box inside that surrounds a tall 1"-wide box with a tiny pincushion in the middle. It is embellished with a doily, buttons, lace, silk ribbon and tiny thread spools.

We also fashioned the Paper Pop-out — constructed entirely from paper.

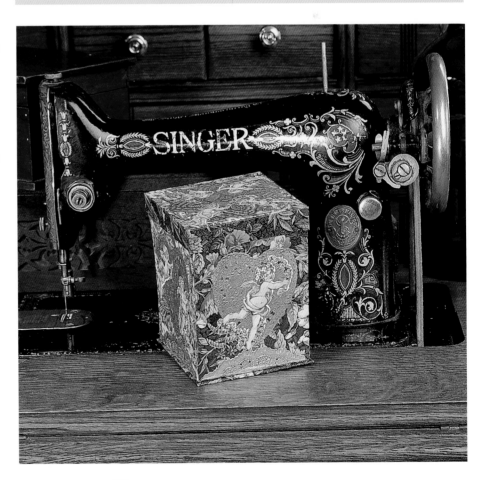

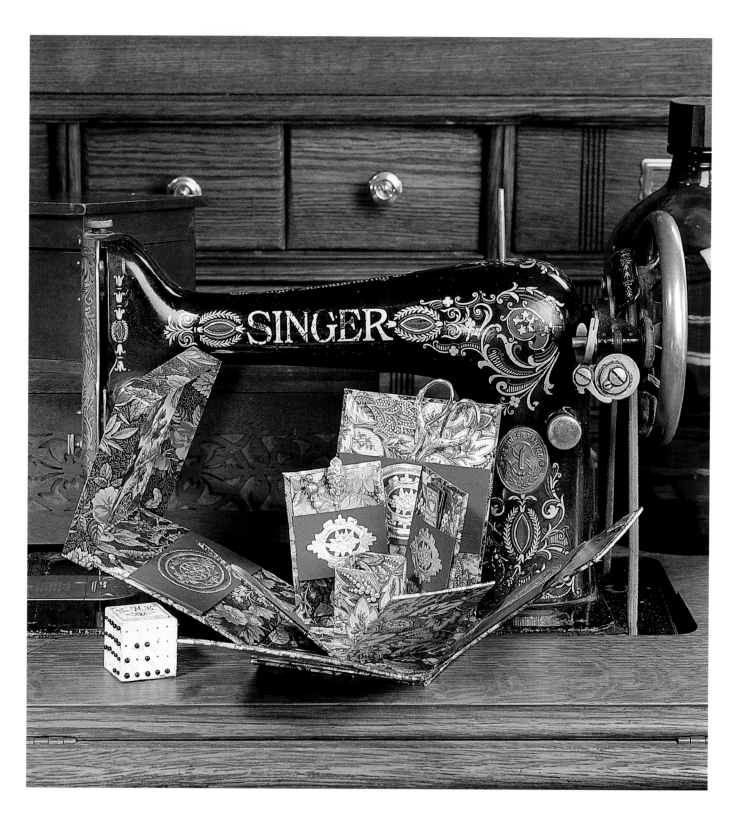

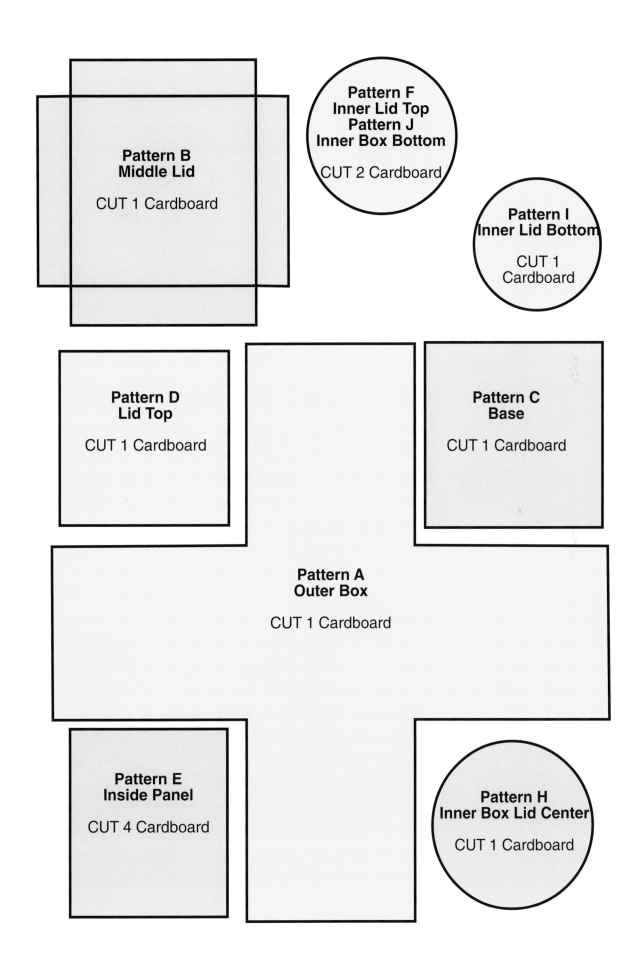

Pattern B
Middle Lid

CUT 1 Cardboard

Pattern F
Inner Lid Top
Pattern J
Inner Box Bottom

CUT 2 Cardboard

Pattern I
Inner Lid Bottom

CUT 1
Cardboard

Pattern D
Lid Top

CUT 1 Cardboard

Pattern C
Base

CUT 1 Cardboard

Pattern A
Outer Box

CUT 1 Cardboard

Pattern E
Inside Panel

CUT 4 Cardboard

Pattern H
Inner Box Lid Center

CUT 1 Cardboard

Friends Forever

Apricot Blossom

MATERIALS
Porcelain doll head and torso
4¼" circle of heavyweight cardboard
14½" x 5½" piece of print fabric for skirt; matching thread
4½" circle of print fabric
14" of lace or tatting
4¼" circle of paper-backed fusible webbing
Stuffing

DIRECTIONS
1. With right sides together, sew a ½" seam 1½" up from bottom and 1½" down from top on short edge of fabric, leaving an opening for stuffing.

2. Press back seams open and press ¼" hem allowance at bottom of skirt.

3. Sew a gathering stitch 1¼" along top edge of skirt.

4. With skirt inside out, insert doll with head toward bottom of skirt. Gather top of skirt tightly around the waist of doll and tie off. Turn doll out.

5. Center paper-backed fusible webbing bumpy side down on wrong side of print fabric circle. Iron on. Pull off paper. Place cardboard circle over webbing and iron to material.

6. Slipstitch circle to skirt bottom, leaving an opening for stuffing and using cardboard as a guide. Stuff firmly and slipstitch opening closed.

7. Embellish by tacking piece of lace or tatting around bottom edge of skirt.

Cornflower

MATERIALS
Porcelain doll head and torso
16" x 6" piece of solid fabric
4" circle of solid fabric; matching thread
12" of matching trim
3½" circle of heavyweight cardboard
3½" circle of paper-backed fusible webbing
Stuffing
Glue

DIRECTIONS
Follow Steps 1 through 6 for Apricot Blossom with the following changes:

1. After gathering skirt, fold and press to make pleats.

2. Use indicated circles and fabrics.

3. Glue trim along bottom of skirt.

Pink Parlour

MATERIALS

Porcelain doll head and torso
½ yard of fabric for dress; matching thread
24" x 5½" piece of white eyelet fabric with one finished edge for pinafore; matching thread
7" x 17" piece of muslin
5½" circle of muslin
4" circle of muslin
5" circle of heavyweight cardboard
5" circle of paper-backed fusible webbing
3 colors of matching 4mm silk ribbon
4 rosettes
Small snaps
Stuffing
1½" basket

DIRECTIONS

Follow directions in Steps 1 through 6 for Apricot Blossom, substituting 7" x 17" piece of muslin for print fabric and using larger circles as indicated.

Woodland Fairy

Doll clothes

All seam allowances are ¼".

1. From dress fabric, cut one 7½" x 25" piece for skirt. Cut the bodice front and back and sleeves from pattern found on page 114.

2. With right sides of one bodice front and two bodice back pieces together, stitch the shoulders. Repeat for the remaining bodice front and bodice back pieces.

3. Place right sides together, matching shoulder seams. Stitch along one center back seam, around the neck, and the second center back. Clip the curved edges. Turn. Proceed to handle both layers of the bodice as one layer of fabric.

4. Stitch a ⅛"-wide hem in the wrist edge of one sleeve. Stitch gathering threads in sleeve cap. Gather the sleeve to fit the armhole. Stitch the sleeve cap to the bodice. Repeat.

5. With right sides together, stitch one bodice side seam and one sleeve. Repeat for the remaining side seam and sleeve. Sew elastic thread ¼" above the hem at the wrist, either by hand or with zigzag stitch over elastic. Gather to fit the doll and secure.

6. Fold the skirt with right sides together and stitch the short ends together to within 2" of the top edge; backstitch. (This seam is the center back; the long edge with the opening will be the waist.) Fold the edges of the 2" opening double to the wrong side and stitch with a narrow hem.

7. Mark the center front of the skirt. Stitch gathering threads along the waist edge. Fold ½" hem double to the wrong side along the bottom edge of the skirt. Hem by hand or machine.

8. Mark the center front of the bodice at the waist. Gather the skirt to fit the bodice. With right sides together, match the center of the skirt to the center of the bodice and stitch.

9. Sew snaps on the center back opening at neck and waist of dress.

10. Weave silk ribbons through eyelets of white eyelet fabric. Finish with French Knots; see page 15.

11. Turn unfinished edges of white eyelet fabric under ¼" and slipstitch. Sew a gathering stitch along long edge. Gather to fit around waist. Sew a snap at waist. Handling ribbons as one, tie a bow in three 1-yard lengths of silk ribbon. Tack bow at waist of pinafore. Cascade ribbon tails around pinafore; see Ribbon Work on page 14.

12. Sew a gathering stitch ¼" around 4" circle of muslin. Gather slightly, stuff and pull threads tightly. Secure to inside of small basket. Hang basket from doll arm.

Woodland Fairy

Woodland Fairy is made to the same dimensions as Apricot Blossom. Four large, wired silk leaves painted with fall-colored acrylics and gold puff paint are glued to her back, creating wings. Smaller leaves embellish her skirt.

Heavenly Helper

Heavenly Helper

This Heavenly Helper is made to the same dimensions as Pink Parlour. A 9" x 18" piece of white glittered tulle is used for the wings. A piece of white 30 craft wire makes them stand. The pinafore is omitted from her ensemble, while a matching piece of gold-trimmed wired ribbon serves for her sash. Gold charms are tacked to the ribbon tails. The bottom of her dress is trimmed with matching braid.

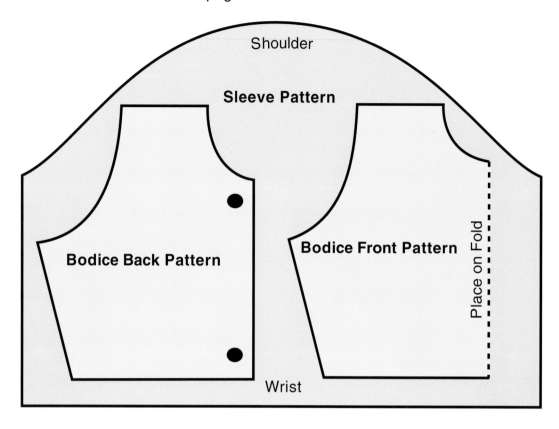

Marble Turtle

MATERIALS

Bronze sculpting clay

5"-square piece of ⅜" plywood

¼ yard of green brocade fabric; matching thread

2 small beads for eyes

Stuffing

Small nails

Hot glue gun and glue sticks

Ceramic cleaning tool or pointed tool

Jigsaw

Drill and small drill bit

DIRECTIONS

1. Using sculpting clay, mold the legs, head and tail. Leave a thin, flat end on each piece that will extend over the top of the wooden base. With a ceramic cleaning tool, draw half-moon scales to resemble turtle skin. Draw a mouth on the head piece and push the small beads in place for the eyes. With a nail, make two holes in each flat end; see Diagram 1 on page 116. Set clay according to manufacturer's instructions.

2. Trace the base pattern found on page 116 onto the plywood. Cut out with jigsaw.

3. Cut fabric according to pattern, adding ⅝" all around. Cover bottom and sides of the wooden base with fabric, folding the edges over ¼" on the top. Trim fabric and glue to base.

4. For the turtle's back, cut out a 9" circle of fabric and sew a gathering stitch around edge. Stuff firmly and gather the thread.

5. When body parts have hardened, glue in position onto wooden base. Using small nails, hammer into base. (The nails will go in easier if you make a hole first with your small drill bit. This will also reduce the chance of breaking parts.)

6. Place the turtle's back onto the base. Folding fabric under, pin into place. Glue fabric over head, legs and tail. After glue dries, hand-stitch back to base for a secure fit.

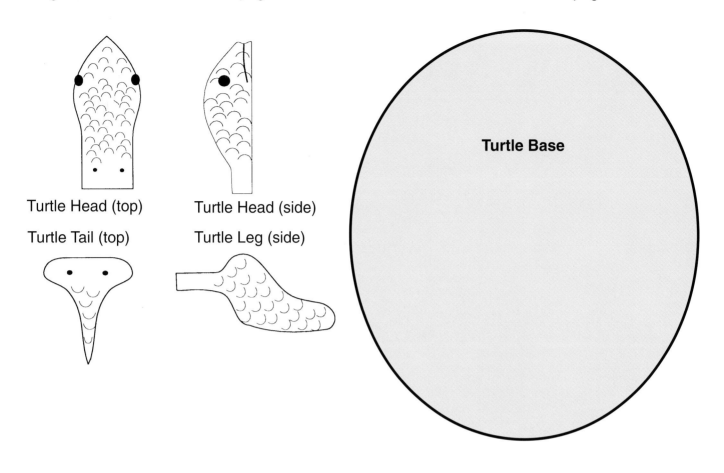

Turtle Head (top)   Turtle Head (side)

Turtle Tail (top)   Turtle Leg (side)

Turtle Base

Woodsfolk

See photo on page 117.

MATERIALS
4" foam core circle
5" empty thread cone
Small Styrofoam ball for head
8" x 5" piece of cream fabric
10" x 12" piece of checked fabric
18" x 2" piece of ivory mesh
3" triangle of brown fabric
Matching thread
Fleece strips
Thin black fabric marker
Strand of small bells
Rice or beans for rattle
Glue gun and glue stick

DIRECTIONS
1. Place large end of cone in center of foam circle. Trace around cone. Cut out inner circle. Bring large circle down over cone, leaving about ½" at the bottom.

2. Wrap fleece strips around cone to make a fat egg-shaped body.

3. Cover small Styrofoam ball with lt.-colored fabric and glue to top of cone.

4. Sew a gathering thread across top of 8" side of cream fabric and pull. Tack around front of neck. (Fabric will not go all the way around body.) Glue bottom edge of fabric to outside edge of large circle.

5. Fold checked fabric in half and drape over body, tucking and tacking to fit body.

6. With piece of ivory mesh, tie in front to make a shawl.

7. Stuff 3" triangle with fleece and whip-stitch long end closed. Sew open end to top of head as a hat.

8. With marker, draw a face.

9. Thread small bells to make a necklace. Secure around neck.

10. Fill cone with rice or beans. Push small circle up into cone to plug.

Country Settee

MATERIALS

12" x 18" piece of plaid fabric
¼" pieces of balsa wood:
    Three 1½" x 1¾"
    One 3" x 5¾"
    One 3¼" x 6½"
½" wood dowels:
    Three 6" for back
    Four 3½" for arms
    Two ½" for armrests
    Four ¾" for legs
6" square of fleece
Four ¼" nails
Glue gun and glue sticks
Pocketknife

DIRECTIONS

Cushion assembly

1. Cover the three small pieces of balsa wood with plaid fabric, gluing fabric edges to underside.

2. Cover largest piece of balsa wood with plaid fabric in the same manner.

3. Fold fleece in half and glue on top of remaining piece of balsa wood. Cover with the plaid fabric.

Couch frame

1. After cutting the dowels into indicated lengths, whittle away strips of wood with pocketknife to give dowels a "log" look.

2. Glue one 3" dowel on top of one short end of largest piece of balsa wood. (These are the lower arm pieces.) Repeat for opposite short end.

3. Position one 6" dowel on top of short dowels toward one end for settee back. Glue a ½" piece of dowel on front end of short dowels.

4. Position two remaining 3" dowels on top of ½" piece of dowel and 6" dowel ends forming upper arm.

5. Glue two 6" logs on top of each other. To complete back, position on top rear of arms and glue.

6. Glue legs to the bottom corners of the largest fabric-covered piece. Turn over and hammer in nails to make more secure.

7. Glue large cushion in place on frame. Glue three small covered pieces along inside back of couch.

Birds On a Line

MATERIALS

¼ yard each of 6 coordinating fabrics
2 yards 4-ply needlepoint cotton thread
Twenty-one ½" round wooden beads
Twelve ⅛" black beads for eyes
Acrylic paints: dk. brown, flesh,
    camel, green, dk. blue
Small wooden birdhouse
Round hook for top of house
One 1" plastic ring
Stuffing
Paintbrush
Old toothbrush
Tapestry needle

DIRECTIONS

All seam allowances are ¼".

1. Cut out one bird from each fabric. Cut two bodies and four wings for each bird from patterns.

2. Sew with right sides together, leaving an opening to turn. Turn and stuff loosely. Stitch opening closed. Glue or tack wing to each side of bird body.

3. Paint seven beads each with dk. blue, flesh, and green. Paint birdhouse roof with green. Paint sides with flesh and paint front and back with dk. blue.

4. Dip an old toothbrush in dk. brown paint. Firmly pull fingernail across bristles to splatter beads and house.

5. Screw hook into top of birdhouse. With cotton thread, wrap tightly around plastic ring. Tie thread in an overhand knot.

6. Thread cotton thread through tapestry needle. String on 3 beads (one of each color), then down through top of one bird, and then 3 beads. Continue this sequence ending with 3 beads. Attach birdhouse; tie off ends.

7. Sew one black bead to each side of bird heads for eyes.

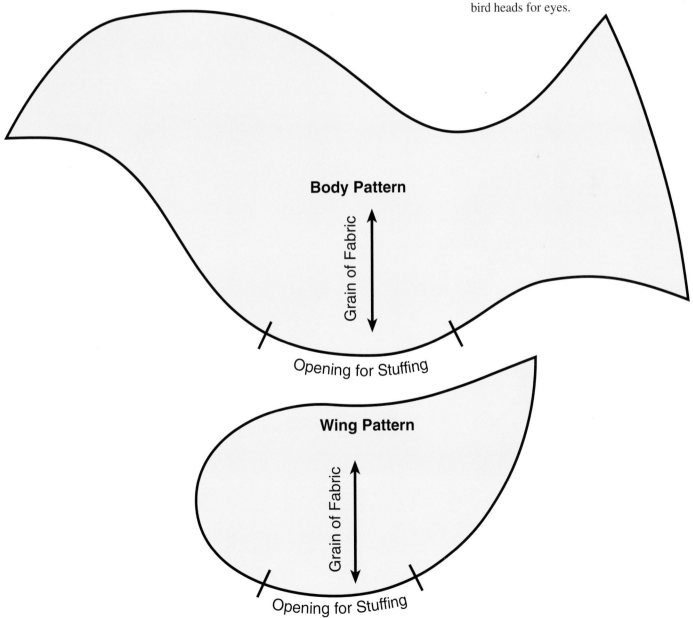

Body Pattern

Grain of Fabric

Opening for Stuffing

Wing Pattern

Grain of Fabric

Opening for Stuffing

Having a Ball and Hanging Around

Having a Ball

MATERIALS
2 ½" Styrofoam ball
4" square of fleece
10 skeins of embroidery floss (various colors)
Sculpting clay
Acrylic paint: white, black
Glue gun and glue sticks

DIRECTIONS
1. Sculpt a cat from clay, making it curved on one side to fit against Styrofoam ball. Set according to manufacturer's instructions. Paint white and highlight with black.

2. Cut away a small portion from one side of the Styrofoam ball so that cat will fit snugly against it. Flatten bottom of ball so it will sit.

3. Wrap ball with fleece square and secure with hot glue. Trim off excess fleece.

4. Wrap floss around ball, covering all fleece. Knot ends to change colors and skeins.

5. Glue cat to side of ball.

Hanging Around

MATERIALS
5" x 7" piece of print fabric
5" x 7" piece of solid fabric
5" x 7" piece of fleece
5" braided trim
30" of cording
Contrasting thread
Sculpting clay
Acrylic paint
1" pin back
Glue

DIRECTIONS
1. Using pattern, cut one chair from both fabrics and fleece.

2. Along the bottom of the print fabric pattern, glue or sew braided trim. In each top indentation of this piece, pin in ends of the cording. (Pull loop of cording within the chair shape to avoid catching it in the seam.)

3. Place fabric patterns right sides together and place the fleece on the solid fabric. Sew around the edge through all 3 layers, leaving an opening at the bottom. Turn. (If you want your chair fluffier, you can insert some extra stuffing at this point.)

4. Hand-sew backstitching, starting at the top of the chair and following the pattern lines. Slipstitch bottom closed.

5. Mold a cat from sculpting clay and set according to manufacturer's instructions. Paint cat. You can glue small pieces of embroidery floss for whiskers. Glue to pin back and attach to chair.

Hanging Around Chair Pattern

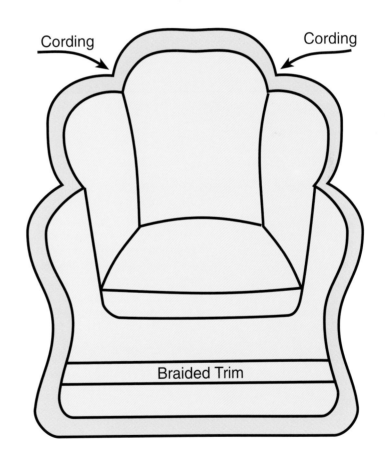

Cording

Cording

Braided Trim

Sunflower Pots

MATERIALS (for one pot)
Small clay pot
8" circle of sunflower-print fabric
1¼ yard of 3" yellow satin ribbon
Stuffing
Tacky glue

DIRECTIONS
1. Turn fabric circle under ¼" and sew a gathering stitch close to edge. Pull thread slightly, stuff firmly and pull gathering closed. Tie off.

2. Apply glue to inside edge of pot. Push cushion into pot. Let dry.

3. Mark 2" sections on yellow satin ribbon and sew a gathering thread; see Diagram 1 below. Pull gathering thread tightly. Glue center of gathered ribbon to pot, arranging ribbon folds to appear as flower petals.

4. Insert Lady Bug pin found on page 13.

Scissor Holder Pattern for Task Basket on page 123

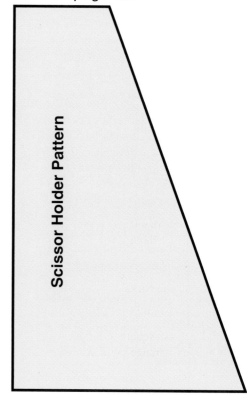

Diagram 1

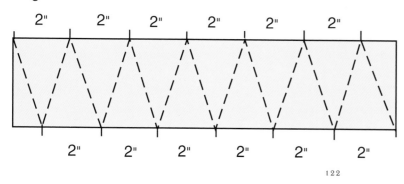

Task Basket

MATERIALS
Large basket
3 small baskets
4" x 6" piece of satin fabric
4" x 6" piece of tapestry fabric
Three 9" circles of tapestry fabric
3" x 5" piece of lightweight cardboard
12" piece of matching braid
Three colors of ¼" silk ribbon
Fleece
Stuffing
Florist foam square to fit large basket
    bottom
Spanish moss
3 to 5 large picks of silk flowers
3 picks of smaller flowers
1 large pick of ivy
Floral wire
Glue gun and glue sticks

DIRECTIONS
1. Cut florist foam square to fit large basket bottom. Arrange moss in bottom of basket.

2. For scissor holder, cut cardboard triangle from pattern found on page 122. Cut fleece from pattern. Cut satin triangle from pattern, adding ¼" for seam. Cut folded tapestry triangle from pattern, adding 1" for seam.

3. Glue fleece to cardboard. Place fleece on wrong side of satin triangle. Pull edges of satin snugly to back side of cardboard and glue. Set aside.

4. Fold tapestry triangle with right sides facing. Sew a ¼" seam along long edge. Press open and turn. Fold top and bottom edges under ¼" and slipstitch.

5. Trim with braid 1" from top and bottom edges. Cut a 3" piece of braid for the hanger. Fold in half with wrong sides facing and stitch ¼" across. Tack at seam inside tapestry triangle.

6. Insert cardboard and satin piece inside tapestry piece. Glue to secure. Use 3 lengths of ¼" silk ribbon to attach scissor holder to large basket handle.

7. Sew a ¼" gathering stitch around each 9" circle of tapestry. Pull threads slightly. For one circle, place a handful of stuffing in center of wrong side of fabric and pull threads tightly. Tie off. Insert "cushion" in one small basket. Glue to secure.

8. To line baskets, turn gathered edge of one remaining circle under to wrong side of fabric and press. Glue turned edge to top inside edge of small basket. Repeat for remaining circle and basket.

9. Position small baskets as desired inside large basket. Glue to large basket. Arrange large silk flowers as desired in basket. Use smaller flowers and ivy to fill empty spaces. Secure with glue and floral wire.

JUNE

S	M	T	W	T	F	S
					1	2
3	4	5	6	7	8	9
10	11	12	13	14	15	16
17	18	19	20	21	22	23
24	25	26	27	28	29	30

Mary Boerens is 7 years old. She enjoys working with watercolors and colored pencils. Her favorite color is lavender and her favorite book is The Cat in the Hat.

A cherished work of art completed by your own little designer can be transformed into a 3-dimensional pin keeper.

MATERIALS
Original artwork
18"-square piece of white velvet
Tan thread
Cardboard tube
Tan fabric dye
Stuffing
Waterpaint pencils
Stiff paintbrush

DIRECTIONS

1. Prepare fabric dye according to manufacturer's instructions. Immerse white velvet square in dye for 30 seconds.

2. Remove and rinse under running water, wringing the fabric to remove excess dye and crush the fabric.

3. Using a photocopy machine, enlarge artwork to a size suitable for a pincushion.

4. Cut out copies, allowing ¼" for seam.

5. Choose the finished style of each piece. (We determined that some of our houses appeared to be round and some looked square. One has a round base, one is rectangular and the other two have gusseted sides.)

6. Measure sides of pattern to determine length of gussets. Cut gusset from velvet to required dimensions. A rectangular gusset is one strip of fabric that provides top, bottom, and both sides of the design and wraps around the front and back piece. A cushion with gusseted sides uses a gusset that provides the bottom and both sides (sides end in an inverted V shape) of the design. A round base is made by using a cardboard tube whose circumference is the same as the doubled length of the bottom of the rounded design.

7. Using copies as patterns, cut patterns from velvet. There should be one front piece, one back piece, and one gusset piece. For round cushion, cut a fabric cir-cle ¼" larger than the circumference of the cardboard tube.

8. For rectangular and gusset-side cushions, with right sides facing, sew gusset around edge of front piece. Sew, with right sides facing, remaining edge of gusset around edge of back piece, leaving a 2" opening for stuffing. Clip corners and turn. Stuff firmly. Slipstitch opening closed.

9. For round cushion, sew, with right sides facing, front piece to back piece. Turn and slip onto cardboard tube. Stuff firmly. Slipstitch fabric circle to bottom of design.

10. Using waterpaint pencils, copy original design onto velvet. If the design is a house, begin by outlining windows, doors, shingles, and other small details with a black or gray pencil. Use colors that match the original design. Match directions of pencil strokes to original design. To blend strokes, use a stiff paintbrush and small amounts of water. Fill in windows with white or yellow pencil.

Seasoned Rocking Chair

See photo on page 128.

MATERIALS
Wood dowels:
    44" of ½" diameter
    22½" of ⅜" diameter
    8" of ¼" diameter
Two 9" x ½" rockers
3¾" x 5" piece of ¼" wood
Two 2" wooden ornaments for top of
    chair
Two 7" squares of fabric
Twine
Lt.-colored paint
Stuffing
Finishing nails
Sandpaper
Wood glue
Saw
Drill and ¼" bit
Hammer

DIRECTIONS
1. Cut the 1½" dowel into two 10½" pieces, two 6½" pieces, and two 5" pieces. Cut the ½" dowel in half (4" each). Cut the 1" dowel into five 4½" pieces.

2. Sand all ends of dowels (except one end of the two 5" pieces) into tips that will fit into a ¼" drill hole. Sand the other two ends of the 5" pieces until rounded.

3. With the 3¾" x 5" piece of wood, place a 4½" piece of dowel across the underside of both short sides. Hammer into place with finishing nails. This will make the seat.

4. With two 4½" pieces, drill two holes in each piece at 1½" intervals. Do not go all the way through. Place each 4" piece vertically in each hole. Glue. This will make the chair back.

5. Lay the two longest pieces of dowel side by side about 4" apart. Place the chair back about 1" down between the two dowels. Measure drill holes, drill, and then glue the chair back in the holes.

6. Drill a hole 2" down from chair back on the inside of each long dowel. This will be used for seat later. Now drill a hole about 4½" down on the front of each long dowel. This is where the arms will go. Drill a hole about ½" in from the rounded end of each round-end piece. These will be the arms. Fit the pointed ends of the arms into the front holes of the long dowels, making sure the drill hole is underneath.

7. With the two 6½" dowels, drill two holes in each at 2" intervals. Fit these two pieces on the underside of the chair arms with the holes facing inward.

8. Place the seat between the chair and glue into the corresponding holes. Glue a 4½" piece of dowel between front legs in bottom hole.

9. Place the rockers underneath the legs and mark drill holes. Drill holes and glue chair onto rockers.

10. Glue wooden ornaments onto tops of chair back.

11. Paint the chair. Let dry and sand off the paint in places to give the chair an "old" look.

12. With right sides of fabric squares together, sew a ¼" seam, leaving a 2" opening to stuff. Turn and stuff. Stitch opening closed. Thread twine through cushion at two corners for chair ties. Attach cushion to the seat.

Vintage Thread Spool

See photo on page 129.

MATERIALS
5" x 7" antique thread spool
Two 4" circles of mat board
13½" x 8" piece of print fabric;
    matching embroidery floss

30" of braided trim
Measuring tape (for embellishment)
8 wooden thread spools (assorted sizes)
Scraps of doily, assorted buttons,
    thimble, needle threader, scissor
    charm
Stuffing
3 tea bags
Wood glue
Wood stain
Brown shoe polish

DIRECTIONS
1. Tea-dye fabric, braided trim, floss, and doily scraps. Set aside. Stain wooden thread spools. Set aside.

2. Remove one end of antique thread spool. Cut holes in center of mat circles to match the diameter of the spool dowel.

3. Fold fabric in half, right sides facing, and sew ¼" seam along short side, forming a tube. Turn. Run a gathering stitch along each end of the tube. Gather one end of tube to fit mat circle. Glue one mat circle to inside of gathered end, leaving center hole visible. Slide covered mat circle hole over spool dowel and glue to spool end. Let dry.

4. Stuff tube firmly around spool dowel. Slide remaining mat circle onto spool dowel. Pull gathering thread to cover mat circle with fabric, leaving center hole visible. Glue fabric to mat circle.

5. Replace wood end of antique thread spool and glue with wood glue. Glue braid trim around top and bottom where fabric meets spool ends.

6. To embellish, glue doily scraps around top of spool. Wrap embroidery floss around assorted stained thread spools. Glue small spools randomly on top of antique thread spool.

7. Rub measuring tape with brown shoe polish for an antique look. Glue to top of antique thread spool in loose loops. Attach scissor charm, buttons, thimble, and needle threader.

A Garden Tuffet

MATERIALS
12" circle of quilted fabric
¼ yard of muslin; matching thread
Two buttons
Acrylic paint for bunny face and heart
Stuffing
Moss
3 tea bags
Thin paintbrush
Long needle

DIRECTIONS
All seam allowances are ³⁄₁₆" using a close tight stitch.

1. Tea dye muslin.

2. Transfer patterns on page 131 to muslin and cut pattern according to notations.

3. With right sides together, sew around legs, leaving tops open. Turn right side out and stuff firmly. Line seams together and stitch across the top. With a needle and thread, make indentations for toes.

4. Sew arms together the same as the legs. Make finger indentations.

5. Sew ears, right sides together, leaving open where noted. Turn and press. Slipstitch opening closed. Tie an overhand knot in center.

6. With right sides together, sew around head and body piece. Turn and stuff firmly. Turn bottom edge under ¼". Slide the legs in place and slipstitch closed.

7. Place an arm on each side of body. Sew a button on one arm and bring needle through body into other arm and button. Go back through again and pull tightly. Secure thread.

8. Paint bunny face and heart from pattern. Glue or sew ears to top of head.

9. Lay quilted circle right side down and place a handful of stuffing on the center of the circle. Pull edges up and tie a 11¾" x 1¾" strip of muslin around top. Tie a bow. Cut out a 6" circle of muslin and place on top of stuffing. Tuck inside and glue in place. Glue moss in basket and glue bunny inside.

10. For Carrot pin, see page 13.

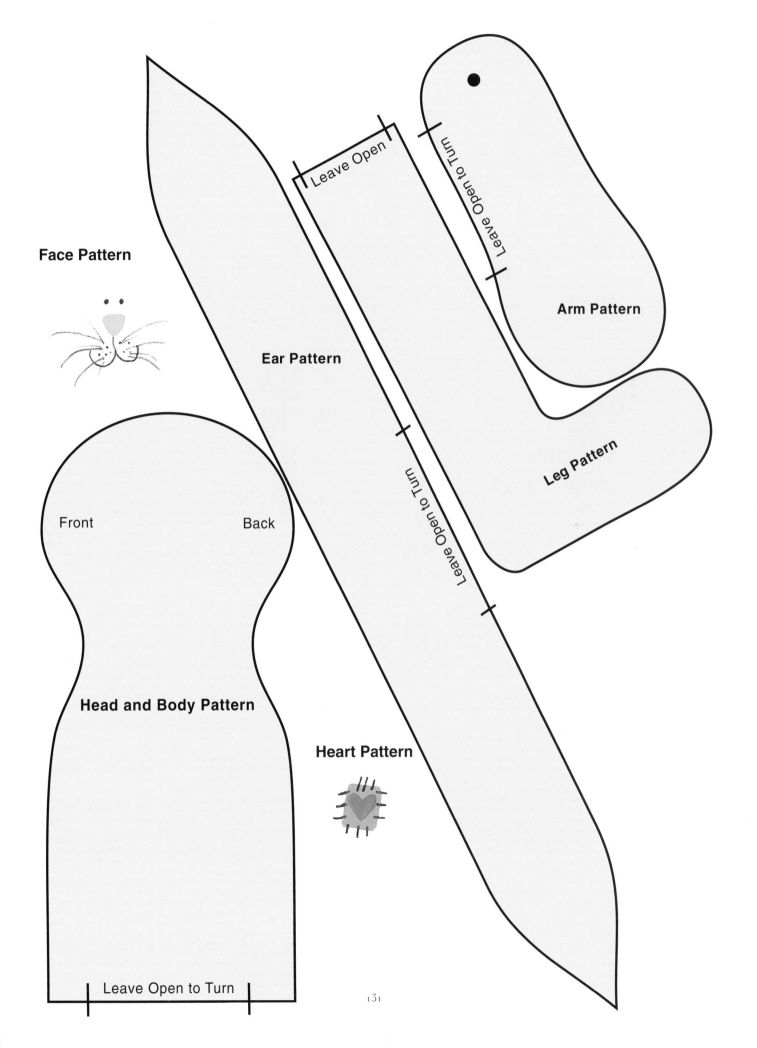

Face Pattern

Ear Pattern

Leave Open

Leave Open to Turn

Arm Pattern

Leg Pattern

Front   Back

Head and Body Pattern

Leave Open to Turn

Heart Pattern

Leave Open to Turn

For the Birds

MATERIALS

30" x 12" piece of ¾" pine
1¼" x 70" piece of wood lath
39" total of ¼" wood dowels
60 craft sticks
9" circle of fabric for pincushion
Stuffing
Acrylic paints
Sandpaper
Wood glue
Wood sealer
Paintbrush
Craft knife
Drill and ¼" drill bit
Saw

DIRECTIONS

1. Cut lath into fourteen 5" pieces. Cut ¼" off the width of 2 pieces. From the pine, cut out the pattern pieces found on page 134 according to notations. Make sure to cut out the "bird hole" from one piece of the birdhouse. Cut base as per Diagram 3 on page 133.

2. Assemble roofs according to Diagrams 1 and 2 on page 133. Supports (craft sticks) for the birdhouse roof are 2 ½" long. Measure 1½" inward from front and back on both sides on underneath of

each roof slope and draw a line. Glue cut craft sticks on insides of lines. These keep the roof from sliding.

For the garage roof, draw a line ¾" from both sides underneath each roof slope. Using the other end of the craft sticks, glue them on the insides of the marked lines. Cut four 1" pieces of craft stick and glue them on top of the other sticks on inside edge.

3. Glue the house pieces together as per Diagram 4 on page 133. Glue the last 4 pieces of lath to the sides of the front and back garage pieces, 2 on each side, one on top of the other. This will form garage sides.

4. Cut dowels into six pieces of 5 ½" to 6½" lengths. Drill holes in bottoms of tree tops. Also drill six ¼" holes in base for tree placement in "yard."

5. Sand and seal all wood.

6. Glue chimney to roof.

7. Cut craft sticks in half for fence. Glue all the way around the base, leaving open in front of house and garage. (Set house and garage on base to see where to glue the fence.) If you have any gaps, craft sticks are easy to cut with a craft knife to make a strip narrower.

8. Paint as in photo or as desired.

9. Glue house and garage onto base.

10. Sew a gathering stitch around edge of 9" circle. Place a handful of stuffing in center and pull gathering thread tightly.

Diagram 1

Birdhouse Roof

1¼"Lath   1"Lath

1¼"Lath   1¼"Lath

1¼"Lath   1¼"Lath

Craft sticks for support

Diagram 2

Garage Roof

1¼"Lath   1"Lath

1¼"Lath   1¼"Lath

Craft sticks for support

Diagram 4

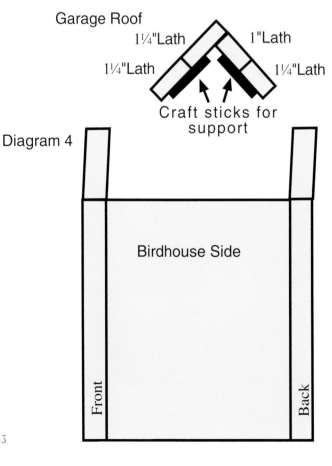

Birdhouse Side

Front   Back

Diagram 3

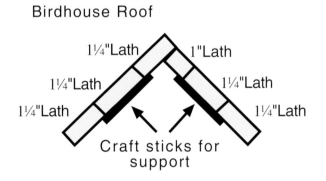

1¼"

Birdhouse Base

6¾"   5½"

8"

6 ¼"   1¼"

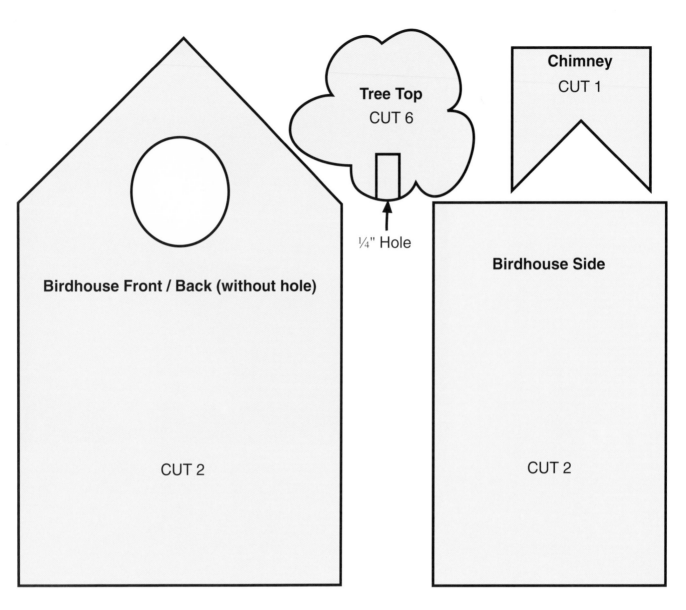

Tree Top
CUT 6

¼" Hole

Chimney
CUT 1

Birdhouse Front / Back (without hole)

CUT 2

Birdhouse Side

CUT 2

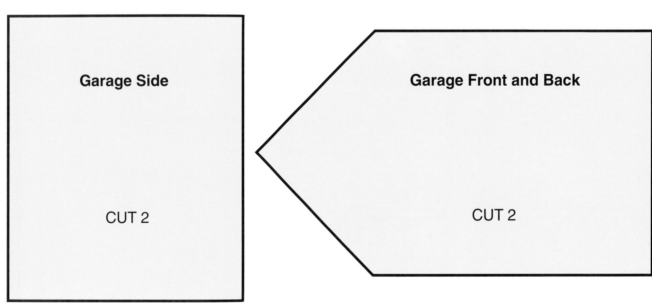

Garage Side

CUT 2

Garage Front and Back

CUT 2

Beehive

MATERIALS

4" Styrofoam ball
4" wooden disk
4 yards of gold velvet cording
2" square of brown felt
Black acrylic paint
Kitchen knife
Glue gun and glue sticks

DIRECTIONS

1. Paint wooden disk black. Let dry.

2. Using kitchen knife, cut off part of Styrofoam ball so there is a flat side measuring at least 3½" in diameter. Roll rounded sides of ball on flat surface, compressing it into a dome shape.

3. Glue flat side of dome to wooden disk.

4. Beginning at the bottom, glue cording 3" to 4" at a time, circling around the dome until completely covered. At top of dome, cut cording and glue end.

5. Round top corners of brown felt square. Whipstitch to lower edge on front side of beehive.

6. Insert Bee pins found on page 12.

Carrot-Collared

MATERIALS

½ yard flower and vegetable print cotton fabric
Scraps of green fabric for ears
White thread
2 black ⅛" beads
2 yards narrow jute
1½" dowel for carrot or 2 purchased carrots
1 spray of green onion grass
Acrylic paint: orange, med. brown
Stuffing
Floral wire
Paintbrush
Drill and small drill bit

DIRECTIONS

1. From print fabric, cut two bodies, two heads, two ears, four legs, and one tail, according to patterns on page 138. Cut one 16½" x 2¼" body inset and one 7" x 1½" strip for head inset. Cut two ears, according to pattern, from green fabric.

2. With right sides facing, sew one head to one edge of head inset, leaving straight edge free. Sew remaining head along opposite edge of inset, matching placement of first head; leave straight edge open. Turn. Stuff firmly. Slipstitch opening closed; set aside.

3. With right sides facing, sew one body to body inset. Sew remaining body along opposite edge of inset, matching placement of first body and leaving an opening. Turn. To make feet in center front of inset, sew a 1" line through all layers of fabric, sewing toward head. Back-tack. Stuff body firmly. Slipstitch opening closed; set aside.

4. With right sides facing, sew two legs together, leaving an opening. Turn. Stuff firmly. Repeat with remaining two legs. Place body, belly side down, on flat surface. Position one leg near back of body with bottom of leg resting on flat surface. Tack leg to body, keeping leg seam centered. Repeat with second leg, matching placement of first leg.

5. Slipstitch head securely to center of body inset 1½" above stitched line of feet.

6. With right sides facing, sew one print ear to one green ear, leaving an opening. Clip curves and turn. Slipstitch opening closed. Repeat with remaining print and green ears. Make a tuck in bottom of each ear; secure thread. Slipstitch one ear to each side of head; see photo for placement.

7. Sew a gathering stitch around edge of tail. Do not cut thread. Gather loosely; stuff. Tighten thread and secure. Tack tail to center back of body inset; see photo for placement.

8. Sew one black bead to each side of head for eyes. Wrap jute 6 times around 3" piece of stiff cardboard. Carefully slip off and tie in the middle with floral wire to make a bow.

9. If you decide to carve carrots from dowels, use a sharp utility knife. Hold dowel so pointed end of carrot is away from you. Position the knife about 2" from end of dowel and whittle to a point. Make two of these—one 2½" and one 2". Using knife, round off carrot top. Drill a small hole in top.

10. Paint carrots with orange acrylic paint. Lightly brush small lines around carrot with med. brown. Glue a 6" piece of floral wire, folded in half, and onion grass in top of each carrot. Let dry. Wrap wire from carrots around center of jute bow. Tie 12" of jute around center of bow and around bunny's neck. Tie in knot under bow.

Greens

MATERIALS

8¼"-diameter circle of floral and vegetable print fabric
Five 6¼"-diameter circles of green cotton fabric
Stuffing

DIRECTIONS

1. To make cabbage head, sew a yo-yo by folding under ¼" and sewing a gathering thread ¼" from fold. Do not cut thread. Gather to make a 2"-diameter opening. Stuff firmly. Tighten and secure.

2. To make cabbage leaf, make a yo-yo with one green circle. Flatten circle so that gathering is at center. Repeat with remaining green circles.

3. Place leaves flat with gathered sides up and overlap edges to make a 7"-diameter circle. Slipstitch together, overlapping edges. Position cabbage head, gathered side down in center of leaf circle; pin in place. Slipstitch bottom edges of leaves to bottom of cabbage head. Fold one leaf up; pinch center. Tack to cabbage head so leaf is slightly puckered; see photo. Repeat with remaining leaves.

Patterns for Carrot-Collared

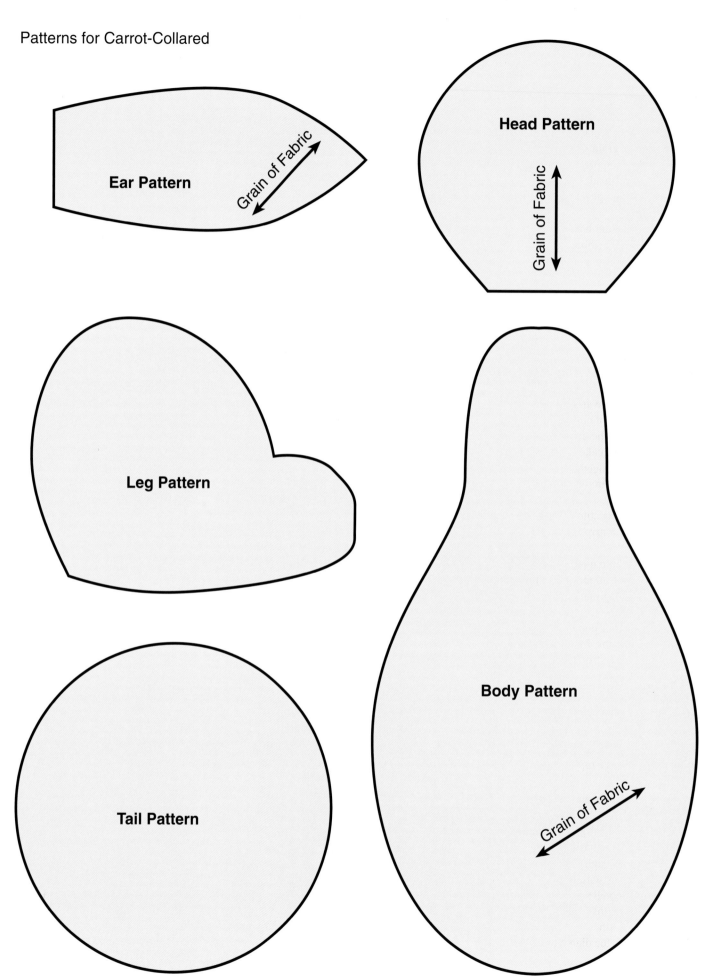

Ear Pattern

Grain of Fabric

Head Pattern

Grain of Fabric

Leg Pattern

Body Pattern

Grain of Fabric

Tail Pattern

Rag Heart

MATERIALS
9" square of needlepoint canvas 14
4 different fabric sraps cut into ¼" strips
   on straight grain
¼ yard of lt. green pre-washed cotton;
   matching thread
Embroidery floss: peach, lt. peach,
   lt. green
1 yard of opalescent bead strand
4mm lt. green silk ribbon
Stuffing

DIRECTIONS
1. Draw a 4½" x 5" heart pattern onto canvas. Randomly work design, pulling silk ribbon, floss, and fabric strips through holes in canvas; see photo. Cut out design, allowing ½" around.

2. Measure distance around outside of heart design. Out of cotton fabric, cut 4"-wide strips twice the distance measured. Seam together to make one long strip. Bring short ends together and stitch a ¼" seam, forming a circular strip.

3. Run a gathering stitch along both long edges of circular strip.

4. Divide strip into quarters and mark with pins on one edge. Gently pull gathering thread along marked edge.

5. Find the quarter points on the design and mark with pins. Match pins on design to pins on strip. Gently pull gath-

ering thread, working extra fabric equally along design and pinning in place. Sew strip to design using a zigzag stitch, making sure to catch the edge of design.

6. Pull gathering thread on other edge of strip until opening is 2" across. Stuff cushion.

7. Cut a circle 1" larger than the cushion opening from cotton fabric. Sew a gath-

ering stitch around circle and gather just until edges curl under. Press edges. Pull out gathering thread and stitch circle over opening.

8. Lay 30" of each color embroidery floss and beads together. Twist. Leaving 6" tails to tie bow, start sewing trim at top center of heart following design edge. Finish at top center. Tie a bow with remaining trim. Cut excess. Knot ends.

Ms. Rosebud and Mr. Fleet

See photo on page 140.

MATERIALS (for one rabbit)
10" x 3½" piece of ¾" pine for base
11" x 5" piece of ¾" pine for rabbit
Woven or ceramic basket:
   5½" to 6½" high
Four 1½" wheels with lugs
¼" wooden dowels:
   Two 5" lengths
   One 7" length
Fabric circle: twice diameter of basket
25" of cording

Embellishments: silk ribbon, dried
   flowers, beads, etc.
1" to 1½" wooden bead for pull string
Stuffing
Wood stain and/or acrylic paints
Gold puff paint pen
Elmer's® Glue
Glitter spray
Glue gun and glue sticks
Drill with ¼" and ⅝" drill bit
Saw

DIRECTIONS
1. Make a color photocopy of Ms. Rosebud or Mr. Fleet, as pictured on pages 141–142. Cut out color photocopy.

2. Using your photocopy, draw a pattern on 11" x 5" piece of pine, being careful not to mark on copy. Cut out with saw and sand edges. Set photocopy aside.

3. With a ¼" bit, drill a hole under hind legs 1" from stomach of wood rabbit. Drill holes on sides of pine base 2" in

from both back and front and going completely through to other side. On the top of the base, drill a ⅝" hole 3¼" in from back center. Drill a hole completely through wood 1" in from front center.

4. Paint and/or stain all wood pieces (except for front side of rabbit) as in photo or as desired. Let dry.

5. Place two 5" dowels through holes on sides of base for wheel axles. Slip wheels onto dowels and glue lugs into lace. Glue 7" dowel into ⅝" hole at back of base. This is where your rabbit will go. Thread

cording into front hole and knot one end. Thread wooden bead onto other end of cording and knot.

6. To decoupage rabbit, mix one part Elmer's® glue with 1 part water. Using sponge brush, apply glue mixture on back of rabbit photocopy cutout. Place on front of wood rabbit and smooth out air and wrinkles. Let dry. With same glue mixture, brush over top of piece and let dry.

7. Using gold puff paint pen, outline the designs on rabbit.

8. If you are using a ceramic basket, paint as desired; see photo. If you are using a woven basket, embellish as desired; see photo.

9. Sew a gathering stitch ¼" around edge of fabric circle. Place a handful of stuffing in center of circle and pull thread tightly. Hot-glue cushion into basket.

11. Place rabbit on top of dowel and fit basket under stomach. Hot-glue into place.

Pattern for Ms. Rosebud

Pattern for Mr. Fleet

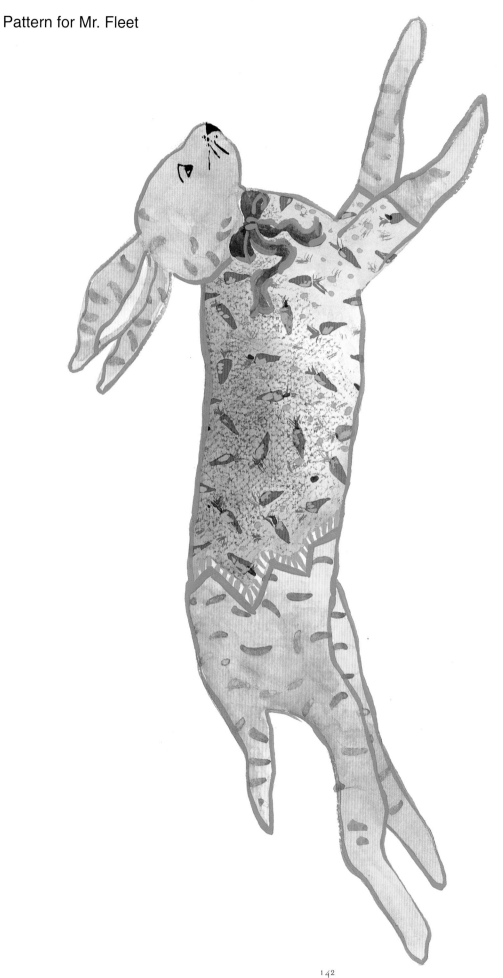

Metric Equivalency Chart

MM-Millimetres   CM-Centimetres

INCHES TO MILLIMETRES AND CENTIMETRES

INCHES	MM	CM	INCHES	CM	INCHES	CM
1/8	3	0.3	9	22.9	30	76.2
1/4	6	0.6	10	25.4	31	78.7
1/2	13	1.3	12	30.5	33	83.8
5/8	16	1.6	13	33.0	34	86.4
3/4	19	1.9	14	35.6	35	88.9
7/8	22	2.2	15	38.1	36	91.4
1	25	2.5	16	40.6	37	94.0
1 1/4	32	3.2	17	43.2	38	96.5
1 1/2	38	3.8	18	45.7	39	99.1
1 3/4	44	4.4	19	48.3	40	101.6
2	51	5.1	20	50.8	41	104.1
2 1/2	64	6.4	21	53.3	42	106.7
3	76	7.6	22	55.9	43	109.2
3 1/2	89	8.9	23	58.4	44	111.8
4	102	10.2	24	61.0	45	114.3
4 1/2	114	11.4	25	63.5	46	116.8
5	127	12.7	26	66.0	47	119.4
6	152	15.2	27	68.6	48	121.9
7	178	17.8	28	71.1	49	124.5
8	203	20.3	29	73.7	50	127.0

YARDS TO METRES

YARDS	METRES	YARDS	METRES	YARDS	METRES	YARDS	METRES	YARDS	METRES
1/8	0.11	2 1/8	1.94	4 1/8	3.77	6 1/8	5.60	8 1/8	7.43
1/4	0.23	2 1/4	2.06	4 1/4	3.89	6 1/4	5.72	8 1/4	7.54
3/8	0.34	2 3/8	2.17	4 3/8	4.00	6 3/8	5.83	8 3/8	7.66
1/2	0.46	2 1/2	2.29	4 1/2	4.11	6 1/2	5.94	8 1/2	7.77
5/8	0.57	2 5/8	2.40	4 5/8	4.23	6 5/8	6.06	8 5/8	7.89
3/4	0.69	2 3/4	2.51	4 3/4	4.34	6 3/4	6.17	8 3/4	8.00
7/8	0.80	2 7/8	2.63	4 7/8	4.46	6 7/8	6.29	8 7/8	8.12
1	0.91	3	2.74	5	4.57	7	6.40	9	8.23
1 1/8	1.03	3 1/8	2.86	5 1/8	4.69	7 1/8	6.52	9 1/8	8.34
1 1/4	1.14	3 1/4	2.97	5 1/4	4.80	7 1/4	6.63	9 1/4	8.46
1 3/8	1.26	3 3/8	3.09	5 3/8	4.91	7 3/8	6.74	9 3/8	8.57
1 1/2	1.37	3 1/2	3.20	5 1/2	5.03	7 1/2	6.86	9 1/2	8.69
1 5/8	1.49	3 5/8	3.31	5 5/8	5.14	7 5/8	6.97	9 5/8	8.80
1 3/4	1.60	3 3/4	3.43	5 3/4	5.26	7 3/4	7.09	9 3/4	8.92
1 7/8	1.71	3 7/8	3.54	5 7/8	5.37	7 7/8	7.20	9 7/8	9.03
2	1.83	4	3.66	6	5.49	8	7.32	10	9.14

Index